# What's Best For Kids



## A Guide To Developmentally Appropriate Practices For Teachers and Parents Of Children Age 4 - 8

by Anthony Coletta, Ph.D.

Published by
Modern Learning Press
Rosemont, NJ

Printed in the United States of America.

Modern Learning Press, Rosemont, NJ 08556
ISBN 0-935493-43-3 Item #521

This book is dedicated to:

Kathi, Michael and Daniel, who
have taught me most of what I know
about human relationships.

They bring joy to my life
and give meaning to the task of
writing a book.

## *Acknowledgments*

I would like to express my thanks and appreciation to the thousands of teachers and parents who have communicated their concerns about children and education to me. In doing so, they provided the stimulus that made this book a reality.

My deepest thanks to Robert Low, Marcia Newfield, and Nancy Hereford. Their support and painstaking reviews of the manuscript kept me focused and motivated. I would also like to thank Bert Shapiro and Linda Skladal for their helpful suggestions and guidance.

Last, my thanks to young children. They continue to teach and remind me what is really important in life.

# Foreword

A century or so ago, when I began my career in education as a grade-school teacher, I often had parents schedule an evening appointment with me to discuss their child's "behavior problems." Being green to education and a bachelor to boot, at first I could only nod sympathetically as each couple described the ordeal to which their youngster was subjecting them.

But as I overcame my awe at being consulted by parents, I cut back on the sympathy and intensified my listening. Though a few children did indeed exhibit behavior problems, it occurred to me that most of the others behaved pretty much the same as their classmates. Finally, I developed a standard response to many of the complaints I was hearing: "As I understand it, your child is acting childishly. Does that sum it up?"

To their credit, most parents caught my point immediately and departed soon after, acknowledging that perhaps their "problem child" was not as hopeless as they had feared. But some missed the irony and applauded my diagnosis: "Exactly! What can we do about it?"

Why is it that, though we never criticize adults for acting adultish, we so readily criticize children for acting childish? It is as if we regard childhood as an inherently defective state, and children as rough drafts sketched by a clumsy God because He doesn't know how to draw grown-ups on the first try. On the one hand, as parents and teachers, we cherish children for their beauty — a natural fact for which they deserve no credit. On the other hand, especially in moments of exasperation, we wish they'd hurry up, knock off this kid stuff, and start behaving like... well, like us.

In a broadly human sense, this adult ambiguity about children and childhood is understandable. Parents have been getting upset about the immaturities of their young ever since Adam and Eve spotted the first signs of sibling rivalry between Cain and Abel, and every one of us has occasionally given way to anger with a child by snapping, "Oh, grow up!"

But when this hair-trigger reaction goes beyond an occasional outburst and becomes educational policy, it's time to analyze the harmful impacts that our adult impatience with childhood can have on the small people who inhabit that distant, secret, tender land.

Along with many of us who work with children, Dr. Anthony Coletta fears that "Grow up!" has indeed been translated into educational policy. He is concerned at the way our society's laudable anxiety for the future of our youngest, and our desire to give them every "advantage" in life's competitive struggle, have been mistranslated into strategies for rushing them out of childhood and into premature youth.

Rather than simply deplore this "Superbaby" trend and its offshoots, however, Dr. Coletta has probed his quarter-century of experience as parent and teacher to document the harm that the hurry-up philosophy can cause to children. Moreover, he presents a thoroughly researched set of guidelines to help adults understand and recognize the developmental stages through which children are passing — and must be allowed to pass through, if they are to mature healthily — and shows how these guidelines can be used to design developmentally appropriate learning and living activities.

The result is a superlative blend of theory and practice that will not only help parents and teachers escort their young charges through a deeply fulfilling childhood, but a volume that should restore our respect for the most powerfully influential, character-shaping period in human life. Through self-evaluation and discipline we adults can revise, alter, and improve our lives. Children, however, have virtually no control over their earliest years, so those of us who guide the young must make their one-and-only voyage through childhood the finest possible preparation for a lifetime of self-discovery. Tony Coletta's ***What's Best For Kids*** will show you how.

Dr. Samuel G. Sava
Executive Director,
National Association of Elementary School Principals

# Introduction to Developmentally Appropriate Practices

*From infancy, Maria's parents treated her as a "super-baby," giving her flashcards and calculator practice, and quizzing her about bedtime stories. When she entered kinder-garten, Maria showed an overall lack of confidence and began falling behind her peers in some subjects. Her mother, who now feels Maria is paying the price of being pushed too early, is attempting to rectify the problem by sending Maria to play therapy classes. "She is full of self-doubts," states Mom, "and will say things like, 'I'm not smart enough.'"*

*Shane lives in a small, affluent suburb where many of the young children attend preschools that teach reading skills. The children also take lessons in tennis, ballet, Suzuki music, swimming, and gymnastics, all before the age of 5. Shane attends a primary school where the second grade class is now taught what used to be a third grade curriculum, due to national reports calling for more "rigor" in the curriculum. Consequently, the amount of homework has increased and group-administered standardized tests have been adopted, beginning in kindergarten. The primary school is now de-partmentalized and has different teachers for different sub-jects, a practice that traditionally began in the middle school. The resulting pressures on Shane have been obvious. Accord-ing to his mother, Shane only cares about "getting through." He says: "School is a war. The playground is a war. The cafeteria is a war. Life is a war."*

*Carl began playing hockey in an organized league when he was 7 years old. At age 8, he told his father he wanted to quit, but the answer was a firm "no." Carl continued playing. As a high school senior, he revealed that for days before a game he would vomit before going to practice. When he drove to games his hand would tremble on the steering wheel and many times he couldn't lace his gloves. His father admits that Carl lacks personal confidence.*

Maria, Shane and Carl are children who have been pushed into experiences before their minds and bodies were ready to cope with them. They are bright and capable youngsters who were pressured to do too much, too soon. They are "stressed-out" and insecure at young ages.

Although their situations may appear to be extreme, increasing numbers of children are under similar pressures. As a result, what teachers and parents are seeing in children between the ages of 4 and 8 are poor attitudes toward school ("I don't want to go to school"), low self-esteem ("I'm dumb, I can't do this"), social aggressiveness, defiance of adult authority, fatigue, withdrawal, and tension.

As a Professor of Early Childhood Education at William Paterson College in New Jersey since 1973, I've supervised many student teachers and had discussions with cooperating teachers regarding the changes they see in the curriculum. These observations andconversations led to my establishing two annual events at the college for preschool and primary grade teachers and supervisors: a two-day "Conference on the Young Child," and a six-week Summer Institute in Early Childhood Education. In addition to my work in New Jersey, I've conducted workshops on developmentally appropriate curriculum for teacher groups in various states.

Over the years, I've heard teachers express increasing disturbance and conflict as they are asked to teach in ways that they know, based on their training and their teaching experience, are not good for kids. They are unhappy with the situation and feel powerless because of dictums from policy makers. Instead of being allowed to utilize their firsthand knowledge of the children they work with, they are forced to follow policies set by remote district supervisors and state officials.

I have also been invited to speak to many parent groups. Starting in 1975, I would get a few requests a year. Since 1985, as parents see kids suffering from pressure, the requests have become non-stop and emanate from a wide variety of neighborhoods. The most popular lecture topics are "Determining Readiness for Kindergarten," "What Is a Good Curriculum for Children?," "How to Manage Difficult Behaviors and Set Limits," and "Improving Self-Esteem."

After a lecture, parents crowd around me with their concerns and questions about the well-being of their children. A typical question is "My son turned 5 in May. I've gone to see the kindergarten. The teacher is demanding, and the curriculum is filled with workbooks and worksheets. I can see there's pressure. Quite frankly, I'm not sure he'll do well. I'm thinking of waiting until he's 6 and more assured to send him to kindergarten, so his self-esteem won't be damaged. What do you think is the right thing to do?"

I would find myself answering this question and hundreds like it by saying, "You have to read this article, that book. There's a video or audio tape that would help explain this." I was referring people to information scattered all over the place, and then I realized that most people do not have time to follow through, even though they desperately want satisfying answers to their questions. I knew what I had to do was put together in one volume the best research and the best evidence we have about child development, along with ways to make use of this knowledge.

It has been demonstrated that the development of children between the ages of 4 and 8 proceeds through a series of stages that are qualitatively different from those of older children and adults. My goal in writing this book is to encourage educators and families to work together in providing what are now frequently referred to as "developmentally appropriate practices" for young children.

Now, just what are "developmentally appropriate practices," so much the trend in education these days that they are humorously referred to as "the D words?"

Developmentally appropriate practices are a process of raising and teaching young children based on an understanding of children's stages of development. These stages vary as to their timing but follow a predictable sequence in each of the four major areas of development -- physical, emotional, social and intellectual. To cite a few specific examples, we will see that young children pass through a series of stages in developing the muscular coordination needed to read and write, in developing the thought processes needed to think logically, and in developing the social skills needed to enjoy being with others.

To implement developmentally appropriate practices, an adult must first have some knowledge of children's stages of development. The acquisition of this knowledge can be combined with sensitive observation to determine a child's stage of development and readiness for different experiences and tasks. Then, a parent or teacher can choose appropriate materials and present them in ways that support a child's current stage, and help to prepare for the transition to the next stage.

In school, developmentally appropriate practices result in a curriculum that meets the individual needs and ability levels of a wide range of students. At home, developmentally appropriate practices result in unstressed kids who respect parental authority and feel good about themselves. In both locations, developmentally appropriate practices result in children who have the ability to acquire skills and concepts, and enjoy the process.

This may all sound like common sense, but unfortunately, in the 1990s many decisions about education and home discipline are based on the needs of adults, rather than on the child development knowledge already in our possession. Too many adults in leadership and policy making positions assume that today's children have somehow advanced and can "handle" learning experiences which were developed for older, more mature children.

A lack of understanding of or attention to child development principles permeates our society. Policy decisions about education are in fact based more on economic, social and political factors than they are on this reliable body of knowledge. This book is an attempt to give people who want to do the best for children a grounding in what is known, so that they can make informed decisions about their personal dealings with children, and bring their influence to bear in matters of public policy.

## A Brief History of the Push-Down Curriculum

How did this current state of affairs evolve? What happened to the good old days when education seemed to work without this kindof intervention? The truth is that in earlier decades we did apply child development knowledge to practice. Then came Sputnik in 1957. The Soviets put a satellite into space before we did, and in response, the United States began an era of educational revamping that has not yet stabilized. Information and teaching methods previously reserved for older children began to be "pushed down" into the lower grades. The pressure to accelerate learning in the early years and make the curriculum more academic increased in the 1960s, because it was felt that our schools were not preparing American children to be competitive in scientific fields.

In the 1970s, the increase of young mothers in the work force, due to a combination of factors including economic conditions and the feminist movement, dramatically increased the middle-class, private preschool population. The subsequent exposure of children to several years of preschool led to demands on the part of parents that the kindergarten curriculum be more advanced and teach more subjects in a formal way. Empirical evidence of the success of Headstart programs for lower income children had shown that these preschool years could indeed be significant for overall development. Why shouldn't middle class children make gains as well?

In the 1980s, intensive education was seen as a solution to the weakened state of American competitiveness in world markets. A much-publicized report issued in 1983, ***Nation At Risk,*** described the lack of America's leadership in technology, commerce, industry and science. On the basis of achievement measurement data from the 1970s, the report showed that our educational standards had dropped drastically and that our youth were performing poorly compared to those of other nations. It concluded that we had not been paying attention to the purposes of schooling and that we must institute higher standards.

This report led to another round of school reforms across America. These reforms were aimed at producing higher standards in the high schools, more uniform requirements, and increased teacher accountability, as well as providing incentives to motivate students, teachers, and administrators to work harder. While the intent was honorable and appropriate to the high school levels, the reforms started filtering down to curriculum planning for the lower grades. What used to be taught in the higher grades was again pushed down into the lower grades. Curriculums were planned from the twelfth grade down rather than from kindergarten up.

Simultaneous with the pressure in schools was the "superbaby" push at home. Achievement-oriented parents were projecting their work ethic onto their kids, wanting them to display productivity as early as possible. Kids were being over-programmed with formal lessons: music, dance, skiing and swimming for children under 8 became the norm for many middle class families. The natural rhythm of childhood -- with unstructured time to wonder, question, share, and acquire skills in a relaxed atmosphere -- became an endangered species in many communities.

The stress, low self-esteem, poor learning attitudes and discipline problems that parents started seeing were a direct result of these changes in primary schools and homes. The movement to teach kids earlier, create standards for each grade level, and hold kids accountable is counter-productive when applied to the lower grades, because of widely variable maturation rates in children under 8. When pressured to take on tasks before they are developmentally ready, kids suffer stress and loss of self-esteem.

Teachers of young children are conflicted because they are often forced to accelerate the curriculums in their classrooms. In a Carnegie Foundation survey of 22,000 teachers, many reported that the pressures in their classrooms are excessive and may result in children "turning off" to learning. To cite an example from Ernest Boyer's "What Teachers Say About Children in America," an experienced Pennsylvania kindergarten teacher voiced her discomfort this way:

"I am extremely concerned about the stress our children are exposed to. The push is for earlier learning — do it faster! The children are not able to learn in a relaxed atmosphere. We no longer have time to read a story every day, do creative dramatics, learn through experimentation, and review previous learning."

The Carnegie survey also found that many early childhood teachers are critical of the negative effects caused by the growing reliance on standardized test scores, which are used to measure student achievement. They feel "locked" into curriculum, scheduling, and test preparation that leaves little time for innovation, creativity or diversity in teaching.

Similarly, many parents feel peer pressures to involve children in experiences that may be developmentally unhealthy. Parents often make decisions based on what other parents allow their children to do. For example, a mother and father enroll their 7 year-old son to play in an organized football league because the child's closest friends and classmates have been allowed to join, and they do not want their child to feel "left out." Or, a 5 year-old is permitted to view videotapes containing sex, violence and scary scenes because neighborhood kids of the same age are allowed to see them.

Dr. James Egan, Chairman of the Department of Psychiatry at Children's Hospital National Medical Center in Washington, D.C., has found that many parents do not want their children to be different from the group. He says: "Parents systematically cultivate an approach that says, 'Do it if everyone else is doing it.' With such an approach, children grow up without the capacity to be different." As they grow older, it should come as no surprise when they defy parental authority. Breaking curfews, poor school performance, promiscuity and bad language are rationalized by saying to parents, "Everyone else does it. You've always taught me to do things because everyone else is doing it." Just like teachers, parents need to make decisions based on information that is known to support rather than undermine children's development, regardless of pressures to do otherwise.

In order to help parents and educators make better decisions about raising and teaching young children, I have summarized the knowledge about child development into six developmentally appropriate practices. What follows is a brief introduction to each practice. A more detailed discussion of the practice and ways to implement it can be found in the chapter of the same number.

## *PRACTICE #1*
## ***Give Equal Attention To All Areas Of Development: Physical, Emotional, Social, and Intellectual***

During the past few years, teachers and parents have seen an increase in the publication of books and magazine articles espousing the importance of intellectual development. Formulas and techniques have been designed to teach young children to read and increase their IQ's. Most of these publications, however, do not discuss the dangers of overemphasizing one area of development to the exclusion of others. It is a myth that if the intellectual side of a child is developed, the rest will fall into place. When the significance of young children's intellectual progress is exaggerated, the growth of essential social, emotional and physical skills may be jeopardized. Physical, social and emotional maturation are closely related to self-esteem. If a child has low levels of confidence in those areas, the progress in school and overall development will be in danger.

As stated in the "Position Statement On Developmentally Appropriate Practice in the Primary Grades" of the National Association for the Education of Young Children (NAEYC), the "failure to attend to all aspects of an individual child's development is often the root cause of a child's failure in school." An overview of the four areas of development is presented in Chapter 1, with emphasis on adult strategies which support each area.

## *PRACTICE #2*
## ***Reduce Stress In Children's Lives***

When each child's unique genetic timetable unfolds in an environment of active and stimulating experiences, children move smoothly from one stage to another of their emotional, social, physical and intellectual development. There is substantial evidence that stress impedes and impairs an optimal progression.

This is especially true when youngsters experience a major setback, such as loss of a parent, divorce, hospitalization, parental drug abuse, or child abuse. It is also true when children are pressured to achieve too early in life.

Stress is created when youngsters are placed into learning experiences which demand more than they are able to give. This stress is compounded by the lack of opportunities to engage in spontaneous, child-directed play. When much of their free time is spent watching television, playing video games, or going from one organized activity to another, children have no healthy release for their tensions. As Marie Winn, author of ***Children Without Childhood,*** has observed, they are "play deprived."

Stressed children suffer emotionally by becoming more selfish, tense, aggressive and greedy. They also become angry, anxious, socially isolated and lonely. Physically, they have depleted energy levels and are more prone to accidents. Intellectually, they find it more difficult to process information and make appropriate decisions and responses. Chapter 2 examines stressors of the 1990s which cause problems for many children. Pressures on the family and school are identified, and suggestions for decreasing and preventing stress are also provided.

## *PRACTICE #3*
## ***Create Respect For Adult Leadership***

Many middle and upper class parents give their children too many material things, while also relaxing limits on inappropriate behavior. This weakens what child development experts regard as a crucial prerequisite for learning: a child's healthy respect for parents' ability to define and enforce household rules with consistency and fairness. If children cannot or do not accept limits set by their parents, they will be unable to accept them from other adults in a leadership capacity. Children who do gain this respect for parental leadership in the early years demonstrate better overall self-control and self-esteem, and are more likely to form positive relationships with teachers and friends throughout the elementary school years.

For some children and parents, the road to respect is paved with what seem like insurmountable odds. Studies show that as many as 15 percent of all children in the U.S. are born with difficult temperaments that cause them to be defiant, stubborn, unhappy, and determined to test the limits of adult authority. These children are very likely to treat parents and teachers with disrespect by refusing to comply with reasonable requests. Child psychiatrist Dr. Stanley Turecki, author of ***The Difficult Child,*** estimates that between two and three million children under the age of 6 can be described as temperamentally difficult. Their parents, as well as parents of children classified as having shy or easy temperamental traits, benefit from using known child management techniques in order to provide positive discipline that results in healthy self-esteem. Chapter 3 shares techniques for building respect for adult discipline.

## *PRACTICE #4*
## ***Protect Children From School Failure At The Beginning***

Children the world over learn to crawl, walk, and then talk. However, not all children are ready to begin walking at age one, and not all of them will be ready to enter kindergarten and successfully cope with the demands of a school environment at age 5. It is a well-accepted fact that young children pass through the same stages of development in a sequential and universal manner, but at different rates of speed. Under the age of 8, children who are comparable in intelligence and age, demonstrate wide variability in skill levels. This means that they require different time frames to learn the "3 Rs."

Children under 8 need to be protected from the enormous damage to self-esteem that can occur if they are repeatedly confronted with tasks that are beyond their maturational levels. A knowledge of developmental stages can attune teachers and parents to observe the wide variation in rates of development among children entering kindergarten. They can then make informed decisions about school placement. In order to flourish, some youngsters may need an extra year in a setting that is matched to their developmental stage. Chapter 4 offers more information on this critical issue of school readiness.

## *PRACTICE #5*
## ***Support A Developmentally Appropriate Curriculum***

Many child development experts and early childhood educators believe that young children need interactive, meaningful and concrete (hands-on) learning experiences. Studies suggest that classes through the second grade which are heavily academic, expect children to sit still for long periods of time, and contain atmospheres that are "right answer" oriented, may harm children educationally and emotionally. Yet an unfortunate trend during the 1980s has been a significant increase in the use of abstract materials such as worksheets in preschools and kindergartens.

Teaching decisions must be based on what is known about how young children learn. Chapter 5 describes the characteristics of a developmentally appropriate curriculum. An effective school should offer an organized, challenging curriculum based on developmental knowledge. This approach creates realistic academic expectations for children, while simultaneously providing an emotionally supportive atmosphere and increasing student's self-esteem.

## *PRACTICE #6*
## ***Support Alternatives To Standardized Achievement Tests***

In many states, standardized achievement tests are used instead of proper assessments to evaluate and place primary grade children into remedial programs or reading groups. These tests are inappropriate for kindergarten, first and second grade youngsters, because children under 8 are not good test takers. They do not possess the level of test-taking skills needed to produce accurate results. School psychologist and author Dr. John Dopyera says that the standard error of measurement is very large for young children.

Standardized testing has the harmful effect of shifting the curriculum toward goals which are easily measurable. Measurable goals should not be the fundamental objective for the early years. High self-esteem and a positive attitude toward learning, along with creativity and social skills, are the most important outcomes of early childhood programs. Chapter 6 describes the problems associated with standardized achievement tests and young children. Alternative methods of assessing students' school progress are described, including performance samples, teacher observation, anecdotal records, checklists, and teacher-made tests.

In a fast-paced world, young children need to be protected from inappropriate situations that may damage their self-esteem and rob them of their right to grow at their own pace. Once parents and teachers become sensitive to the unique characteristics of children under 8, there is so much they can do to support healthy development.

Each chapter that follows contains very specific strategies for supporting young children, along with explanations of the principles and evidence that underlie these strategies. Appendix A is a kindergarten readiness checklist for parents, and Appendix B provides an informal teacher observation checklist for 4 to 5 year-olds. Appendix C contains a checklist of developmentally sound practices at school and at home, while Appendix D is an extensive compendium of books, articles, organizations, and audio and video tapes that are helpful in raising and educating children in ways that support their developmental needs.

This book grew out of my discussions with thousands of concerned teachers and parents over the past 16 years. My hope is that it will provide the information needed to help such adults do what is best for the children in their care.

*Practice* 1

# Give equal attention to all aspects of development: emotional, social, physical, intellectual

*Jennifer's mom began teaching her to read at age 2. Her third birthday was celebrated with a computer and software programs that required a second grade reading ability. With lots of tutoring, Jennifer was reading by age 3 1/2. At this point, her parents went to the nursery school director and insisted that Jennifer be moved out of the 3 year-old class and in with the 4 year-olds. Since Jennifer was shy and might be overwhelmed by the more active older children, the director questioned the change, but reluctantly agreed.*

*Jennifer turned 5 on September 28th and missed the October 1st cutoff date for kindergarten entrance. But once again her parents insisted that she be placed with older children. The Board of Education agreed to their demand. Currently in first grade, Jennifer is reading above grade-level but is physically unable to keep up with the other children. During recess, while most of her class plays tag or kickball, she prefers less physical activities, either alone or with one other child. She has few friends and prefers to talk to the teacher during social times like free play and snack time.*

While Jennifer's parents are concerned and want the best for her, they have mistakenly assumed that a child's intellectual development and academic achievements are what matter most, and that the emotional, social, and physical areas of development will take care of themselves. Right now this thinking may seem correct, but in the long run it will prove harmful to Jennifer.

Jennifer's growth, like all children's, is interrelated -- a lack of development in one area affects progress in another. Children who have trouble making friends (social) are likely to be unhappy (emotional) and may demonstrate less energy on the playground (physical). In the classroom, they may find it difficult to concentrate on the subject at hand (intellectual). Although the social, emotional, physical, and intellectual areas are often discussed separately, in actuality they are intertwined and cannot be isolated from each other.

It is therefore important to encourage development of "whole" children -- to nourish positive self-esteem, physical coordination, a curious mind, and social competence. Dr. Asa Hilliard, Professor of Urban Education at Georgia State University, notes that children are "willing to try out new things, new toys, new relationships, new space, new people, and one would expect to see this growing over time. The child's innate curiosity is learning's chief asset." Balanced attention to all four areas of development is essential, because it is the achievement of a range of skills and attitudes that leads to the creation of well-rounded, healthy personalities. Following is a discussion of each developmental area along with specific strategies for nourishing it.

## Emotional Development

**Goal: Self-esteem**

**Characteristics: Trust, autonomy, initiative, industry**

In the book, ***Childhood and Society,*** Erik Erikson has outlined the stages of emotional growth, and the major developmental tasks children face at each stage. In order for children to become emotionally healthy, characteristics such as trust, autonomy, and initiative need to be achieved with the support and encouragement of adults.

Trust is the basis for all healthy human relationships. In infancy, trust is learned when the baby's needs are responded to. "If babies are to trust us," says Professor Ron Lally, member of the Day Care Committee of the National Center for Clinical Infant Programs, "we must quickly answer their cries of distress." Knowing this, it is especially important that infant day care facilities provide trained, dependable caregivers. Without proper attention, mistrust may develop and negatively affect both current and future emotional growth. For instance, adults who are unable to trust others are often unsuccessful in developing intimate and satisfying relationships.

By ages 2 and 3, children need to acquire autonomy. They learn independence by mastering self-help skills such as eating, dressing and bowel/bladder control. Giving them opportunities to make modest choices about materials and toys in a safe home or school environment also fosters autonomy. Doubting one's ability, on the other hand, hampers autonomy. Doubt can develop when adults' demands are inappropriate for the child's age -- for example, if adults pressure children to become toilet trained before they are ready, or to sit still for long periods of time.

Between ages 3 and 6, Erikson says that the main goal is encouraging initiative. One way to nurture initiative is by giving children choices about projects and allowing them to act on those choices by creating and building with materials. Children acquire a sense of direction and purpose when encouraged to pursue an idea, focus on it, and bring it to completion. Adults lend support to children's choices and extend initiative when they arrange stimulating environments, ask questions and make suggestions.

Conversely, children become frustrated in their attempts to develop initiative when they are placed in overly structured situations and given few choices. They need guidance and firmness when necessary, together with physical space, hands-on materials, and the freedom to explore and investigate. If these conditions are not available, children are apt to feel guilt.

Feelings of guilt arise when children behave in ways that are contrary to the expressed wishes of adults. For example, if consistently admonished to "sit still and be quiet" or asked "Why do you have to ask so many questions?", children are given the message that active exploration and curiosity are "bad" behaviors. They feel at odds with themselves when their self-starting ideas are continually discouraged. Without opportunities to choose activities, interact with materials, and feel a sense of individual accomplishment at completing a task, a passivity and lack of faith in their ability to create and solve problems may result. In their adult years, they may become dependent on others and be reluctant to act on their own.

During the elementary years (ages 6 to 12), Erikson states that children must develop industry by successfully learning the "tools of the culture." These tools include skills and attitudes such as learning the 3 R's, taking responsibility for homework, and realizing that completing home and school tasks can bring about a feeling of personal satisfaction. If a child has difficulty learning for whatever reason, a state of inferiority may develop. This, in turn, will impede the formation of a positive identity during the teenage years and into adulthood. On the other hand, children who have developed trust, autonomy, initiative and industry are likely to have a strong sense of self-esteem throughout their childhood years.

## *Self-Esteem*

Self-esteem is a child's personal evaluation of his

or her own worth. It is an attitude children have about themselves that develops as a result of how they are treated by family members, teachers, and friends. According to Michael Knight, co-author of ***Teaching Children To Love Themselves***, the way in which significant others perceive children's accomplishments determines how children feel about their personal abilities.

Children with positive self-esteem gain confidence in themselves, while those with poor self-esteem remain convinced that they are not worthy of affection. This view is heavily dependent on adult expectations and communication, both spoken and unspoken. It is therefore vital that adults express love, concern, and respect for the children in their care.

The ability of parents and teachers to build and protect self-esteem is especially crucial when children are 5 and 6 years of age. At these ages, unrealistic home and school expectations may lead children to question their abilities. Dr. David Elkind, author of ***Miseducation: Preschoolers At Risk***, states that this may be a time when "the child's budding sense of competence is frequently under attack, not only from inappropriate instructional practices ... but also from the hundred and one feelings of hurt, frustration and rejection that mark a child's entrance into the world of schooling, competition, and peer group involvement." Like Erikson, Elkind believes that difficulty with the 3R's during the early childhood years may eventually lead to a sense of inferiority. Self-esteem can be impaired by adults who repeatedly ridicule children's attempts at initiative or place children in situations that set them up to fail. Because young children's self-esteem is delicate and vulnerable, they are more at-risk than an adult when faced with tasks that are developmentally beyond them.

Children simply do not possess the defense mechanisms that adults use to protect their self-images. When adults find themselves in learning situations they do not understand, they are likely to criticize the competence of the instructor or the quality of the reading material. They may say, "This teacher is not explaining the material clearly enough," or "This textbook is poorly written." However, when 5 and 6 year-old children are given school tasks which are beyond their level of understanding, they are likely to blame themselves and say "I'm stupid."

As children grow older, they will be confronted with many experiences that could damage their self-esteem. These experiences may involve harsh or abusive treatment by adults, lack of space and quality in their physical environment, or a rigid and accelerated school curriculum. For example, in "Declining Perceptions of Competence," a study of classroom environments, researchers Deborah Stipek and Denise Daniels found that kindergarten children perceived their own abilities as lower when the curriculum inappropriately emphasized academics.

Self-esteem may be affected further when children are criticized by their peers, coaches, or teachers for being "different." Bullies may single them out for ridicule, personality conflicts may occur, and sibling rivalry or unfair treatment by a brother or sister may intensify.

We cannot prevent all the wounds that children are likely to suffer, but we can focus on certain behaviors that help them maintain and increase self-esteem. By understanding the stages of emotional development and responding appropriately, adults can support young children and help them make the transitions needed to prepare for an emotionally satisfying life.

## *Strategies for Fostering Emotional Development*

**Frequently reappraise the expectations you have about a child.** Children can surprise us by suddenly showing new skills. Evaluate your behavior and the emotional atmosphere it creates in the classroom or the home. Ask yourself the following questions:

Do I avoid comparison and competition between children?

Do I give more positive attention to children who are attractive and intelligent?

Do my interactions with children help them feel more attractive and intelligent?

Do I express respect as well as love and concern?

Do I discipline without damaging self-esteem?Am I careful not to speak negatively about children when they are within hearing distance?

Do I have any underlying resentments toward them that need to be resolved?

Do I occasionally take time to engage in activities with children and not just direct them to the activity?

**Give children individual praise and recognition for accomplishments.** In her article, "The Development of Self-Concept," Hermine Marshall, Associate Professor of Elementary Education at San Francisco State University, further recommends helping children learn to evaluate their own accomplishments. However, children also need to be reminded that our love and concern is ultimately unconditional, that we are proud of them regardless of their achievements.

**Encourage 3 to 6 year-olds to engage in sociodramatic play.** This type of play is an important ingredient in developing positive self-esteem, because children acquire positive feelings about themselves by pretending to be powerful figures. Charles Wolfgang's book, ***Growing and Learning Through Play,*** contains many play ideas for preschool and kindergarten children.

**Take the time to listen.** Careful listening shows children they are important. Solicit and respect their ideas and suggestions. Demonstrate a non-judgmental attitude and listen with acceptance when they express problems. Hear the feelings behind the words. Acknowledge statements of hurt, anger, disappointment, or perceived unfairness. To improve listening skills, read ***How To Talk So Kids Will Listen & Listen So Kids Will Talk,*** by Adele Faber and Elaine Mazlish.

**Build confidence by encouraging mutual solutions to problems.** When a conflict arises, ask, "What do you think we should do about this problem?" When possible, allow children to work out their own solutions.

**Encourage positive thinking.** Help them develop a "can-do" attitude. In his book, ***Hide Or Seek,*** psychologist Dr. James Dobson suggests teaching children that negative thinking and constant self-criticism accomplish nothing. Use "Peanuts" comic strips to discuss Charlie Brown's view of his own inferiority to make the point.

**Give them the strength to believe in themselves.** When children are called names, insulted, or ridiculed by others, remind them of all the things they do well and that "no one can make you feel badly about yourself, unless you allow it."

**Teach children to compensate for their weak-**

**nesses by focusing on and developing their strengths.** Help them identify what they do well and what they want to improve. Provide the necessary resources, coaching, time for practice, and encouragement.

**Determine if children are early or late readers.** Only one to three percent of all young children read with comprehension upon entering kindergarten. Most do not show an interest in the mechanics of reading until ages 6 or 7. Since the ability to read is highly related to the development of self-esteem, make sure they are given enough time to learn. Do not force them to read before they are ready. For more information, read the article, "Communicating With Parents About Beginning Reading Instruction" by Dorene D. Ross. I also discuss these issues further in the section of this chapter on Teaching Reading Based on Children's Vision, and in Chapters 2 and 5.

**Discipline without impairing self-esteem.** Be clear about behaviors that are permitted and those that are not. Set and describe firm limits and the consequences of ignoring them. Follow through immediately on what you have said.

**Highlight the value of the child's ethnic or racial group.** Select books that describe admirable people from different ethnic populations. A list of such books can be obtained by writing to the Council on Interracial Books for Children.

## Social Development

**Goal: To feel satisfaction both when relating cooperatively with others and when engaged in solitary activities**

**Characteristics: Knowing how to enter a play situation, initiate conversation, take on a role and use one's imagination. Being able to be aware of one's own needs and also be responsive to the needs of a playmate.**

During the preschool and primary years, parents and teachers face the task of socializing children. For the most part, children learn social skills by watching siblings, peers, and adults as they interact. Children's ability to exercise self-control -- to share, wait for a turn, cooperate and speak politely -- develop at least as much by imitating the people around them as by following instructions.

Studies show that children move through a series of developmental stages along the road to adult-type friendships. They do not achieve immediate and lasting intimate friendships during the preschool and primary years. Robert Selman, Associate Professor of Education at Harvard Graduate School of Education and author of ***Making a Friend in Youth***, says that the first stage of friendship can be referred to as "momentary playmateship." At this stage, around ages 3 to 7, friends are whomever one is playing with at the time. The next stage, known as "one-way assistance," occurs sometime between ages 4 and 9. Children at this stage believe that a friend is someone who does things to please them. They have difficulty realizing that a relationship involves give and take -- "sometimes we do what you want to do, and then we do what I want to do."

Gaining an understanding of the reciprocal nature of friendship is an important development that evolves between ages 6 and 12. At this stage, children understand that friendship is a two-way street. When children become adolescents they enter the stage of "intimate, mutually shared relationships." They are better able to experience friendship as an ongoing relationship in which two different people with separate wants and needs learn to cooperate.

However, for some children, this sequence of social behaviors is impeded. There may be a variety of reasons for delay, including a child's innate temperament. Three basic types of temperaments — easy, shy and difficult — are described by Dr. Stella Chess and Dr. Alexander Thomas in ***Know Your Child***, the report of their study of 133 infants from birth to age 30. (This important work is discussed more extensively in Chapter 3). Children born with difficult or shy temperaments may have trouble moving smoothly through the developmental stages of socialization. Temperamentally difficult children are often in a negative mood, and exhibit intense reactions to situations. They become overly aggressive and explosive with their peers, which makes it difficult for them to make and keep friends.

Social skills may also be difficult to learn due to shyness, according to Marion Hyson, Associate Professor of Family Studies at the University of Delaware. Children born with a shy disposition are particularly vulnerable to shyness at certain developmental points -- at 4 or 5 years old, and again in early adolescence. Shyness is often a normal response to social experiences that children perceive as overwhelming. They withdraw temporarily to gain a sense of control. In her article entitled, "The Shy Child," Alice Honig explains that shy children are not necessarily at risk for psychiatric or behavior problems. Shy youngsters with positive self-esteem tend to catch up to others quickly. But children who exhibit extreme shyness, lack social skills throughout school, and have poor self-images may need help from adults. Numerous suggestions for coaching such children and modeling appropriate behaviors appear at the end of this section.

When children are ostracized because of physical problems, a "funny" name, or some other characteristic that makes them different, they have trouble moving smoothly through the developmental stages of socialization. This is true for children who consistently suffer frustration, rejection, or failure for whatever reason. Being left out and feeling rejected may lead some children to exhibit aggressive behaviors and others to withdraw.

Young children who have difficulties learning social skills suffer feelings of isolation and loneliness. Loneliness is not to be confused with being able to be content alone, but is rather a feeling of alienation and the lack of feeling loved and lovable.

Low achievers often suffer feelings of low self-esteem because of their struggle to learn the 3 R's. As a result, they may turn inward and avoid interacting with others or asking for help, because they fear negative or judgmental responses.

In her book, ***Smart Children With School Problems,*** Priscilla Vail explains that bright, high-achieving children are also vulnerable to loneliness, because they are "right-answer" oriented and so are likely to correct and criticize classmates. In addition, their teachers may view their questions, such as "Why do we have to do this?", as a personal attack.

Children who fall into any of these categories need adult intervention, in order to move through the stages of social development without suffering long-term damage due to their particular circumstances. It is imperative to address this area of growth. In a study reported in ***Psychological Bulletin***, Jeffrey Parker and Steven Asher found that students who lacked social skills, and were rejected or neglected by their peers, were likely to become high school dropouts or delinquents, or experience mental health and loneliness problems in adulthood.

To prevent such problems from occurring, adults can help children develop social skills and empathy. When children understand their peers and know how to interact with them, their social development can proceed far more easily.

Sociometric studies show that popular children are more outgoing, sociable, and friendly than others. They frequently engage in cooperative play and social conversation, and they refrain from verbal and physical aggression. Much of this behavior can be learned with help from adults.

There are three main ways to teach social skills and empathy to children. Immediately **praise** children (positive reinforcement) for demonstrating positive behavior. For example, acknowledge acts of sharing and cooperation. Second, **coach** children in how to participate, how to cooperate, and how to communicate with others. It is especially important to teach youngsters how to make statements expressing kindness and appreciation. Finally, **model** positive social behaviors. Demonstrate nurturing and caring behaviors, and have children do the same. Also have them point out acts of compassion from live peer models and those on television or in films.

The following pages contain more detailed suggestions for supporting children's social development.

## *Strategies for Fostering Social Skills and Empathy*

### Social Skills

**Teach children social-skill phrases to use, such as "Can I help you build?" or "Can I play too?",** suggests Alice Honig, Professor of Child Development at Syracuse University.

**Teach children the secrets of being a good friend -- one "who makes others feel special about themselves,"** recommends Phillip Zimbardo, author of *The Shy Child.* A good friend is more "sociocentric" than "egocentric" in considering the desires of the other person.

**Teach children to smile at others, listen to others and make eye contact.** People who are not shy smile often at other people, listen attentively, and respond with words. Their successful social behaviors can provide a model for children to whom this does not come naturally. Adults can talk about these successful strategies, ask questions, and provide gentle reminders. Helpful tips should not be one-time-only lessons, but rather coaching that adults provide up through adolescence. Advice to not interrupt others in the middle of a sentence may be more necessary for a temperamentally difficult child, whereas making eye contact is a breakthrough for a shy child.

**De-emphasize competitive games and increase games of cooperation.** Emphasis on winning and losing is discouraging to all young children. For shy youngsters, it is terrifying and can promote inaction; for temperamentally difficult or aggressive children, overly competitive games can exacerbate behaviors that are already volatile. A good source of cooperative games is *The New Games Book* by Andrew Fluegelman.

**Encourage a sense of humor by reading humorous jokes, riddle books, and silly rhymes.** Children make friends more easily when they share humor.

**Identify the children with whom a shy child interacts positively, and make arrangements to get them together for play or an interesting project.** Also, encourage a shy child to play with one child at a time or with a younger playmate.

**Teach "productive peer-interaction patterns" in situations as they occur,** advises Dr. Lillian Katz, Professor of Early Childhood Education at the University of Illinois. This means showing kids how to share, cooperate and solve problems. For temperamentally difficult children with a history of aggression, it is too difficult to break the negative cycle alone and an adult is needed as a coach.

**Use a "sociogram" to incorporate the concept of peer modeling among the students in a classroom.** By asking questions such as "Who would you like to sit next to you?" or "Who do you consider to be your best friends?", a teacher can determine the most and least popular children in a classroom. With this information, groups can be created for special projects by mixing the most popular students with the least popular. Such groupings allow less popular children to learn from the socially effective behaviors of the popular children.

**Use the activities found in *Learning The Skills of Peace-Making* by Naomi Drew, and *Cooperation In The Classroom* by David and Roger Johnson.** Both these books provide ideas for teaching and encouraging social skills in the classroom.

**Limit the amount of television time.** Children often substitute the comfort of TV and video games for more challenging social interactions. See the discussion of the effects of television on children in Chapter 2.

**Encourage children to speak for themselves.** Allow them to call a store to find out the price of a toy, or order their own meals at a restaurant. At school, when a child complains that another child's behavior hurt him, encourage the child to verbalize his needs and feelings to his peer.

**Counteract children's ridicule of others.** If a child has an unusual name that other children ridicule, make that name a household word. Use it frequently and with positive connotations. Use the same positive reinforcement technique to alter the perspective on anything about a child that is regarded as unacceptable because it is different from the norm.

**Maximize physical appearance.** If a child is physically unattractive, focus on a new hairstyle, attractive clothes, and a healthy body and skin. Make efforts to control any weight problems so that the child gets positive feedback from others.

## *Developing Empathy in Children*

Although children under the age of 7 are often unable to empathize or understand another person's emotions, empathy tends to increase with age. To a great extent, children's consideration for the welfare of others depends on the existence of a nurturing bond within the parent-child relationship. Therefore, the time parents spend with their children, as well as their ability to communicate love, are important factors in developing the ability to empathize.

Adults support the development of empathy when they:

**Model an empathic attitude.** Caring is "caught" more than it is taught.

**Teach children that their behavior toward others is important.** Recognize and applaud caring and considerate treatment of friends.

**Give children responsibilities for the care of living things like pets and plants.**

**Read books that deal with kindness and generosity.** Examples include ***Fiona's Bee*** by Beverly Keller, ***Shoeshine Girl*** by Clyde Robert Bulla, ***A Chair For My Mother***, by Vera B. Williams, ***Freckle Juice*** by Judy Blume and ***The Velveteen Rabbit*** by Margery Williams.

**Confront behavior that is insensitive to others.** Psychologist Julius Segal, author of ***Compassionate Kids***, writes that his mother watched games in the street unfolding and reprimanded any of her children who mistreated others. Help children to understand the benefits of compassion, and the scars that unkind behavior leaves.

**Be alert to tendencies to over-please.** Dr. Segal also cautions us that some children can care too much. While parents may feel their child may be "too good to be true," the child's underlying motivation is not always altruism, but anxiety. These children need to talk about their concerns. They need to know that they are "loveable and capable" and do not need to constantly please others.

**Include caring in the curriculum.** School has an important part to play in the development of empathy in children. In a 1983 study, "Children Helping Peers: Altruism and Preschool Development," researcher Carolyn Simmons concluded that teaching and modeling nurturing behaviors increases children's empathic responses toward others. Cornell University psychologist Urie Bronfenbrenner, author of ***Two Worlds of Childhood***, has for years advocated a "curriculum for caring," whereby children would not only learn the concepts of kindness, they would participate in its practice. After several visits to the Soviet Union, Bronfenbrenner recommended the use of a Soviet educational policy known as "shevstvo," in which each class takes responsibility for rearing a group of children at a lower grade level. Older children become big brothers and sisters for the younger children. They teach them to play games, help with homework, and often walk with them to and from school. To follow-up each morning, the teacher asks the older students questions like, "After school yesterday, what did you do that helped someone young, old or sick?"

# Physical Development

**Goal: Large and small muscle coordination, plus visual coordination, which enables children to develop competence and independence**

**Characteristics: A sense of balance; ability to walk, run, and skip; ability to throw, catch and hit a ball; ability to write, cut, draw; ability to focus and sweep the eyes from left to right.**

The physical development of young children is

highly impressive. During the first 2 years of life, a baby quadruples his or her birth weight and more than doubles in height. Growth between the ages of 2 to 6 slows somewhat but is far from stagnant. On average, preschoolers gain four to five pounds and grow about three inches each year. They gradually acquire such essential life skills as the ability to feed and dress themselves, and to control bowel and bladder movements.

The biological process of physical maturation, combined with opportunities to practice movement, determines the progress children make in gross and fine motor skills. Gross-motor abilities involve the use of large muscles, while fine-motor skills employ small muscles in the hands and fingers. Control over the large muscles occurs before small muscle control because, as Yale University psychologist Edward Zigler points out in his book, ***Children: Development and Social Issues***, fine-motor development is more dependent on brain maturation than is gross-motor muscle development.

It takes time for most preschool children to acquire fine-motor skills, because they lack the control of small muscles needed to execute such tasks. Skills such as running, skipping, and throwing a ball are acquired easier and sooner than cutting with scissors, holding a pencil, and writing. Practice in gross-motor activities should therefore always precede fine-motor work. Children struggling with fine-motor activities, such as writing letters and words on paper, need more practice with gross-motor movements such as writing letters in the sand and in the air.

A closer look at the development of handwriting follows, along with information about the development of children's vision and its effects on writing and

## *Handwriting*

In many homes and schools, 3, 4 and 5 year-olds are told to "stay within the lines" when writing letters and numbers. Empirical evidence shows that most young children cannot successfully comply with this request. I often see this happening in kindergartens I visit. It usually occurs before an "open house," when a teacher wants to display examples of children's writing. Some of the 5 year-olds simply cannot comply. They get frustrated, cry, and start developing a negative attitude towards writing in general. This is because they first need to practice sweeping strokes by painting and writing large letters with thick brushes, pencils, felt tip pens, or chalk. Writing at the chalkboard, on unlined paper, or at an art easel, is the best preparation for eventually being able to "stay within the lines."

Children show a consistent, age-related progression in their writing abilities. Rhoda Kellogg's classic work, ***Analyzing Children's Art***, describes this progression from scribbles to recognizable forms like circles and lines, and then to representational figures. Repetitive practice in one stage of motor development helps children master one skill and then move on to another. The following milestones are approximate and vary with each child:

Children begin scribbling by age 2.

They scribble vertical lines at age 2 and then start drawing horizontal lines.

They create recognizable forms (circles and lines) by ages 3 and 4.

They draw circles bottom-up and clockwise (age

4), before they draw them top-down and counter-clockwise (age 5).

They draw representational figures (people and homes) at ages 4 and 5.

They are interested in letters and printing their names at some point during their fifth year.

Reversals of letters (d for b) is normal between the ages of 5 1/2 to 6 and usually disappears during the sixth year. (NOTE: A child who does not outgrow reversing letters and numbers, or continues to see them upside down, may be dyslexic. Dyslexic children display an overall difficulty with words, along with speech problems, the inability to hear sounds accurately, and, often, memory lapses. For information on teaching methods that help dyslexic children, write to The Orton Dyslexia Society.)

The goal of handwriting instruction is to encourage children to write legibly in comfort. It should not be a frustrating experience. Children are ready to benefit from the teaching of handwriting only after they can easily use crayons, scissors and pencils in a variety of activities. They should be able to copy simple geometric shapes with a firm and stable stroke, and hand dominance (whether right or left handed) should be clearly established. Charles Temple, co-author of ***Language Arts: Learning Processes and Teaching Practices,*** states that "handwriting instruction usually begins during the first semester of first grade. By then most children are ready to profit from instruction while others would best be delayed until second grade."

According to Temple, "play writing," or "pseudowriting," is the most powerful indicator of handwriting readiness. Children will play write shopping lists for grocery stores or letters to friends. Gradually, their play writing progresses in stages from scribbling to one-letter, invented spellings, such as "i d t m s," which stands for "I do it myself." The third stage involves two- and three-word sentences. These stages usually surface during the kindergarten and first grades. By second grade, most children are writing full sentences.

Legible handwriting should be of no concern during creative writing lessons. At such times it is vital that children feel free to use invented spelling and to write, scribble, or draw their thoughts without fear of judgment.

## *Teaching Reading Based on Children's Vision*

Children's vision, like their fine and gross motor control, improves in a predictable manner through a series of developmental stages. For example, according to Dr. Louise Bates Ames, author of ***Is Your Child in the Wrong Grade?***, children who are 3, 4, and 5 have limited visual skills. The majority of them are not ready for formal reading.

Most 4 and 5 year-olds are interested in recognizing words, especially those with personal meaning, such as their names. By age 5, most children can focus on a word, but may not have the ability to sweep the eyes from left to right. This is a skill which usually emerges between 6 and 6 1/2. Parents and teachers need to be sensitive to the limited visual abilities of beginning readers and avoid the formal teaching of skills in isolation. Research on early literacy suggests that when parents use an informal approach and provide a language-rich environment, learning to read and write becomes easier for children.

An informal approach involves reading good literature, telling stories, conducting stimulating discussions, and encouraging children to retell stories. This approach is more effective than teaching through isolated letters, flashcards, or rote memorization of the alphabet. Studies by reading expert Delores Durkin, author of ***Children Who Read Early,*** concluded that parents who attempted to teach reading formally were not as successful as parents who responded to children's requests for information about reading.

In his book, ***Miseducation,*** David Elkind states that only one to three percent of all young children are reading with comprehension before entering kindergarten. These children possess a strong desire to read and will teach themselves if not taught by adults. However, the majority of children are not interested in the mechanics of reading (a phonics approach of teaching sound-symbol relationships) until after the age of 5 or 6. Says Elkind: "We miseducate them if we introduce such mechanics before children show any inclination in that direction."

Because most 6 year-olds are better able to sweep their eyes from left to right, they are more likely to benefit from more direct, formal instruction in reading. Still, some 6 year-olds may need more time for their eye muscles to coordinate before they can read well. Richard Kavner, optometrist and author of ***Your Child's Vision,*** believes that many reading problems occur because instruction is given to children who are not developmentally ready. For children maturing more slowly, he suggests that "it would be better if they were held over during the very early years." These children need additional opportunities to enhance their perceptual skills.

Other optometrists such as Harold Wiener, author of ***Eyes OK, I'm Okay,*** report that children are generally far-sighted until age 6, which is nature's way of protecting them from over-focusing. Children who are unable to focus their eyes clearly on a page are not ready for reading instruction and will be under considerable stress if expected to perform. Dr. Richard Apell, co-author of ***Preschool Vision,*** says "For the child who is not ready to read, three things show up under stress: loss of the ability to focus; loss of the ability to point (converge) the eyes; and the possibility of poor eye movement."

Researchers have found that the six muscles of each eye must coordinate precisely to focus on near objects and to produce only a single mental image. At 6 years of age, the visual mechanism is still unstable. Lillian Gray explains in ***Teaching Children to Read*** that some children do not develop the ability to focus on objects at close range until they are 7 or 8 years old. However, approximately 85 to 90 percent of children are developmentally ready to read at age 6 1/2.

## *Strategies for Fostering Physical Development*

**Make sure that school personnel create and maintain movement experiences within the curriculum.** Movement activities should be an essential part of any program serving children from ages 4 to 8. Since practice is an important element in developing motor skills, children should play outdoors or in a gymnasium for a minimum of twenty minutes or a half hour every day, with a balance between vigorous child-initiated play and teacher-directed movement experiences. Such programs should include body rolls, crawling, skipping, running, balancing, and rhythmic activities.

**Encourage children to engage in creative movement experiences.** This enables them to explore their bodies in space, connect body to mind, and develop confidence and pleasure in their ability to move. Some suggestions for adult interventions are: "Pretend you are a cloud moving on a windy day." "Pretend you are a seed growing into a plant." Include music in the background.

**Before teaching letters and numbers, encourage experiences with painting, clay and collages.** Gross motor movements are developed in these activities.

**Read *Feeling Strong, Feeling Free: Movement Exploration for Young Children* by Molly Sullivan and *Leap To the Sun* by Judith Peck.** These books contain good ideas for movement activities at home and school.

**Support development of children's eye-hand (visual/motor) coordination through ball games and drawing activities.** Have children throw balls or bean bags at targets, trace around figures or complete mazes, and play games such as "Statues" in which the leader's position is copied by the children.

**Begin children's writing experiences with large body movements.** When children show an interest in letters and numbers, avoid giving them pencils and lined paper. Instead encourage them to practice writing letters in the air, in sand or with a flashlight in a darkened room. Also, use a watergun outside and create words with water. Allow children to write letters and numbers on large sheets of butcher paper, using large strokes with thick crayons, large paint brushes, and magic markers. The paper can be placed either on the wall or the floor. Children will respond positively to unstructured, open-ended materials and the use of gross motor muscles, because this suits their developmental stage. Until the age of 7, they will not normally work in a more confined manner (pens, pencils and lined paper) unless forced to do so.

**Encourage children to have direct, sensory experiences with symbols.** Use clay to sculpt the shapes of the letters. Buy or create sandpaper letters, and encourage children to "feel" each letter by running the index finger over the outline of each letter. Learning for young children depends on sensory input. Therefore, having children experience the shape and feel of letters by modeling them in clay or tracing them on sandpaper will improve their learning, because it stimulates their senses. Another good idea is to shape dough into letters, bake them and then eat the letters.

**Encourage children to write about their experiences even when it appears as scribbles.** Children's scribbling is intended as writing and lets them practice the necessary movements. Scribbling progresses from random markings to left-to-right progression, and then slowly begins to take the shape of letter forms.

**Arrange a writing center in the classroom.** Include felt-tipped markers, large and small crayons and pencils, chalk and a chalkboard. If possible, include a computer or typewriter. Make available lined, but mostly unlined paper, index cards for recording "my very own words," and both white and colored construction paper for making books. An alphabet chart in easy view helps children identify and shape letters they may need for writing. Also display children's writing, including first scribbles, on a bulletin board. ***Literacy Development in the Early Years: Helping Children Read and Write,*** by Leslie Mandel Morrow, elaborates on how to create a writing center.

**Obtain appropriate software for a computer included in a writing center.** Word processing programs, such as ***Muppet Word Book*** (for 4 and 5 year-olds) and ***The Writing and Publishing Center*** (includes graphics for ages 6 to 8), motivate young children to write and "publish" their own stories. Once the children are shown how to use the programs, they can create and illustrate their favorite words, as well as turn their own stories into books. ***The High/Scope Survey of Early Childhood Software 1990*** includes an evaluation of 435 computer software programs for young children.

**Consult with a family physician.** A child who frequently displays one or more of the following eye-related symptoms may need corrective lenses: rubbing the eyes, squinting, looking with one eye, eyestrain headaches following a period of reading, or choppy eye movements that make it difficult to follow words in a sentence from left to right.

**Start with familiar materials.** To increase the skills of focusing and left-to-right scanning, use a child's favorite story book. Beginning at the top left side of the page, point to all the words that begin with a certain letter. Allow use of the index finger to follow words across the page.

## Intellectual Development

**Goal: To establish the foundation for logical thought**

**Characteristics: Ability to learn by manipulating concrete materials and experiencing situations that are personally meaningful**

Swiss psychologist Jean Piaget has described a series of stages through which children's thought processes evolve over the years. During the first two years of life, children are in the **sensorimotor** stage, which means their thinking is totally dependent on seeing and touching objects again and again. They understand the concept of a "cup" simply by using one. This stage evolves into the **pre-operational** stage, which is characterized by the rapid acquisition of language. At this point, a child understands the word "cup" as well as being able to use the object. This stage continues from about age 2 to ages 6 or 7. Next comes the **concrete operations** stage, which lasts to about age 12. During this stage, children can mentally manipulate symbols, such as classifying cups as part of a group of objects used for drinking.

Children between the ages of 4 and 8 are thus evolving from the pre-operational stage to the concrete operations stage. Their brains have not yet sufficiently matured for them to be able to mentally engage in the more complex symbolic operations required when applying rules (as in reading, spelling, phonics and basic arithmetic). Pre-operational children have to use their hands and act on objects in order to gain an understanding of concepts in the world (i.e., temperature, size, comparisons). The hands-on experiences they have at the pre-operational stage are critical in facilitating the development of logical thought.

Piaget described the thinking of 2 to 7 year-olds as "transductive reasoning," to differentiate it from the deductive or inductive reasoning that characterizes logical thought. Transductive reasoning allows children to see a relationship between two or more thoughts when there is no relationship. For example, on an afternoon when a child does not take a nap, he or she may say, " I haven't had my nap so it isn't the afternoon." When a child associates good feelings with a stuffed animal, he or she thereafter believes the stuffed animal caused the good feelings. If a 4 year-old falls, he may blame it on the sidewalk, or if he is injured, he may blame a child who was not even near him.

Winnie the Pooh is well known for his pre-logical, transductive reasoning. In one honey and bee adventure, Pooh, after visiting Rabbit, eats so much honey that he gets stuck in the door and immediately blames it on the narrowness of the door. Rabbit, who is often clever and a bit mean, sternly advises Pooh that "...it all comes of eating too much."

Universally, 2 to 7 year-olds display certain cognitive characteristics that seem to be at the root of their transductive reasoning. They are **egocentric**, **perceptual**, and **animistic**. Egocentricity causes children to see themselves at the center of the universe and believe that theirs is the only point of view. To the pre-operational child, cars are for "me" to ride in, grass is for "me" to walk on, and snow is for "me" to make a snowman. On the negative side of this thinking pattern, a child might believe that it was something he or she said that caused Mom and Dad to separate.

According to Robert Smith, author of "Early Childhood Science Education: A Piagetian Perspective," egocentric thinking can lead to misinterpretations of natural phenomena. When asked, "Why does it get dark out, 4 or 5 year-olds may respond, "because I have to go to sleep." Or they will say, "The sun moves when I move." This is why concrete materials and active learning experiences are so important during these years. The opportunity to explore, manipulate, question, recall, compare, and label form the foundation of children's ability to think logically and make distinctions between beliefs and reality.

Pre-operational children's thinking is considered perceptual because they are easily fooled by appearances. Judgements about quantity are based on how objects look. They might say a beach ball will sink in water because it is so large, not taking into consideration that it is also light. Also, they lack the ability to understand conservation, in that they believe the amount of an object changes when its shape changes. For example, a 4 year-old child will agree that two rows of five dominoes each, arranged parallel to each other, are equal. If the same dominoes are rearranged so that the bottom row is a circle and the top row a straight line, the child will say there are more in the straight line "because it is longer."

Young children are also animistic thinkers. They believe inanimate objects possess a consciousness and are capable of coming to life. The moon and ocean "sleep" at night and the sun "wakes up". Donald Peters and Sherry Willis, authors of ***Early Childhood,*** reproduce a 4 year-old's animistic thinking in this conversation with an adult:

Adult: What does it mean to be alive?
Child: It means you can move about, play — that you can do all kinds of things.
Adult: Is a mountain alive?
Child: Yes, because it has grown by itself.
Adult: Is a cloud alive?
Child: Yes, because it sends water.
Adult: Is wind alive?
Child: Yes, because it pushes things.

Adults can help children progress through the stages of intellectual development by providing hands-on materials, encouraging social interaction, and creating situations in which "meaningful" learning can occur through literature or play. Many adults also assume they can help speed children's intellectual development by teaching them to read at an early age. However, the ability of young children to read with comprehension and enjoyment is learned through a series of stages, and rushing or truncating these stages can have harmful effects. While there are a small number of children who show a natural inclination to read at an early age, this is a result of the child's developmental process rather than any parental activities.

During their preschool years, children learn to enjoy listening to stories read to them by adults, which should be done every day. Jim Trelease, author of ***The New Read-Aloud Handbook***, reminds us that attachment to an adult is an important part of the process of learning to read.

The next stage begins at ages 4 and 5, when children are able to acquire meaning from a story by memorizing and telling the story to an adult or other children. The third stage involves demonstrating a knowledge of concepts about print, such as identifying upper and lower case letters, pointing to words as they are read, and showing an understanding that print rather than a picture carries the message. Teachers can easily assess children's concepts of print by using Marie Clay's "Concepts About Print Test."

Once children have successfully moved through these three stages, they are ready for instruction in phonics -- the relationship between words and the sounds they represent. Preferably, this will be done through meaningful stories and game-like activities. Some children will be ready for phonics instruction at age 5, but most will not be ready until age 6.

Throughout the 1980s and into the 1990s, many parents and even some teachers have unknowingly blocked progression through the stages of learning to read, by introducing phonics before children have demonstrated the ability to memorize and retell stories, as well as understand concepts about print. Drilling young children in phonics through the teaching of isolated letter sounds, which have no connection to meaningful words and stories, increases the risk that the children will develop negative attitudes toward learning and themselves.

More specific suggestions for supporting young children's intellectual development follow.

*Strategies for Fostering Intellectual Development*

**Develop language ability and interest in reading by reading to children and providing many books suited to their age, interest and reading levels.** Refer to *The New York Times Parent's Guide to the Best Books for Children.*

**Provide opportunities for children to develop oral language through meaningful experiences.** Experiencing is only half of learning -- discussions about experiences are a critical part ofunderstanding them. Play with friends and pets can stimulate the ability to use language, as can trips to new places. They enable children to clarify concepts and digest their feelings.

**Be a good model of language.** Go out of your way to explain things to children and answer their questions. The use of prepositions is related to conceptual understanding (i.e., near the stove, by the window). Try to be conscious of speaking in whole sentences.

**Provide concrete materials for play.** Locate hands-on objects such as blocks, Legos, Tinker Toys, science materials and art supplies. Create collections of things that can be classified, such as leaves, seeds, coins and butterflies. Read ***The Book of Think: Or How To Solve A Problem Twice Your Size*** by Marilyn Burns. Teachers will find a lot of suggestions in *The Critical Thinking Handbook: K-2* by Richard Paul.

**Teach math and reading through game-like situations.** Refer to *Games for Math* by Peggy Kaye and *Teaching the 3 Rs Through Movement Experiences* by Anne Gilbert.

**Encourage children to solve their own problems as they occur during play situations.** For example, the adult can provide alternative choices that the children then discuss and select. Let them figure out what to do when two children both want to play the role of the teacher.

When teachers and parents use developmentally appropriate practices to help young children grow intellectually, emotionally, socially, and physically, they support the learning process. In the next chapter, I will explore the negative effects of home and school stressors on children's ability to learn, and discuss what can be done to cope more effectively with stressors or prevent them from occurring altogether.

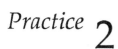

*Practice* 2

# Reduce stress in children's and adults' lives

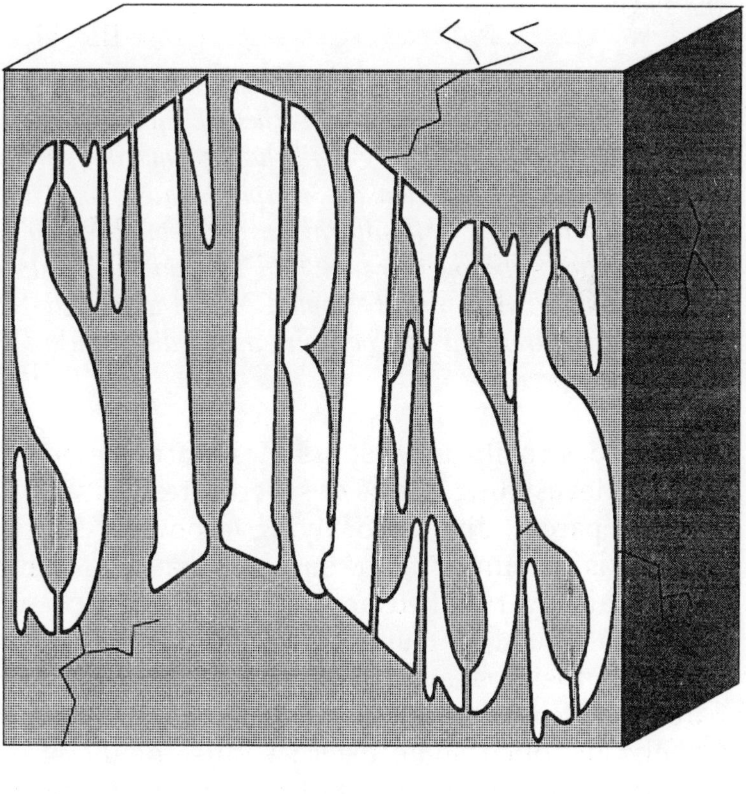

*Ronald's parents are very busy people with demanding occupations. His father, a systems analyst, and mother, an attorney, are so involved with work commitments they have little time or strength left over for parenting. Since he was 3 months of age, Ronald has been enrolled in day care. During evenings and on occasional weekends, neighborhood women have been hired to attend to him. They allow Ronald to watch as much television as he wants, which amounts to about 5 1/2 to 6 hours a day. When he was 4 years old, his parents arranged for a violin teacher to come to the house every week to give him hour and a half lessons. Starting in the second grade, he requested and was allowed to play organized football and soccer.*

*Currently in the third grade, Ronald has problems with self-control and getting along with others. Unfortunately for Ronald, discipline and setting limits have primarily been the responsibilities of his caretakers, simply because he is with them most of the time. And, since his parents want to enjoy the brief time they have together with him, they do not set limits on his behavior. As a result, Ronald cannot accept control from other adults and can be quite demanding with both teachers and peers.*

Ronald is a child under stress. He is not experiencing the devastating effects of severe stressors such as loss of a parent, divorce, or living in poverty, but instead he is encountering the stressors that occur when parents are overworked and set premature achievement goals for their children, without setting proper limits on their behavior. I have encountered many parents of "Ronalds" following my lectures. They have usually identified some external cause of the stress signs they see in their child. It's hard for them to see that a change in their own behavior might be helpful.

This is not to say that all stress is unhealthy. All

children inevitably experience stress in the form of demands on their bodies and minds. Much of it will be productive and maturing, such as the tension of acting in a class play for the first time. Problems may develop, however, when young children experience simultaneous and continuous stressors from several different sources. In a study of children's responses to stress, Michael Rutter found that psychiatric disorders more than double when children experience two or more severe risk factors together. For example, youngsters may be part of a bitter divorce battle and suffer poverty as well.

Because stress is a very subjective circumstance, being "under stress" is often a personal evaluation made by the individual experiencing the stressful events. Marion Hyson, Assistant Professor of Individual and Family Studies at the University of Delaware, notes "A minor disturbance may be devastating when one's resources are depleted; conversely, the availability of support may turn a possibly stressful experience into a routine challenge." Children clearly need guidance from teachers and parents in learning how to identify and cope with stressful situations.

## Stress and Its Signs

How can we tell when young children are under stress? Pediatrician Dr. Benjamin Spock, acclaimed author of ***Baby and Child Care***, tells us that when children are consistently placed in situations that are too stressful, they suffer **emotionally** by becoming more selfish, tense, aggressive and greedy. The emotional consequences of chronic stress have been further identified by researcher Camille B. Wortman, who concluded that excessive stress can cause overwhelming feelings of anger.

Dr. David Elkind, Professor of Child Study at Tufts University and author of ***The Hurried Child***, states that stressed children suffer from what Sigmund Freud called "free floating anxiety," a restless and irritable feeling that is difficult for the child to clearly identify and describe. Such anxiety is experienced particularly by children involved in separation and divorce, and by those who watch violent television programs and films for which they are not emotionally prepared.

**Socially**, overly stressed children may demonstrate extreme behaviors such as aggressiveness or withdrawal from friends and family. This may contribute to an inability to make and keep friends, and eventually lead to feelings of isolation. Child development specialist Pamela Roby, author of ***Child Care — Who Cares?***, has identified loneliness as one of the greatest hazards facing children in our society.

**Physically**, stressed children are more prone to accidents and illnesses, and they may suffer ulcers and increased headaches due to muscle tension. Child Trends, a research group in Washington, D.C., estimates that 35 percent of children's health problems are due to stress. Barbara Kuczen, author of ***Childhood Stress: How To Raise A Healthier, Happier Child***, reports that stressed children are three times more susceptible to infection and illness. Because they are apt to be anxious or irritable, they are two and one-half times as likely to have an accident, and the possibility of their requiring hospitalization increases eightfold. They may also be reluctant to get involved in after-school activities because of depleted energy levels. Researcher James Tanner has stated in his book, ***Foetus Into Man***, that in extreme cases stress causes a decrease in the brain's production of growth hormone, preventing some children from growing.

**Intellectually**, stressed youngsters are easily distracted and find it difficult to concentrate on school work. Clare Cherry, co-author of ***Is The Left Brain Always Right?***, states that increased tension in children can significantly decrease the perception of incoming information. Stressed children find it more difficult to process information and make appropriate decisions and responses. Cherry believes that the amount of learning can be substantially increased by teaching young children relaxation techniques. When children are relaxed, information travels through the system more accurately and efficiently.

Children under stress often display a combination of these behaviors. Dr. Pat Fosarelli, assistant professor at Johns Hopkins School of Medicine, has found that stress is the cause of many psychosomatic illnesses seen in children today. The more stress kids are under, the more they have headaches, stomach aches, and chest pains that have no organic cause. They have sleeping problems, they daydream, they cannot concentrate, and they have difficulty learning.

The first step toward helping children under stress is to recognize the symptoms. Negative emotions such as anxiety, anger, and despair are clues that children are unable to handle the demands in their lives. Here are some specific behaviors to look for:

unable to concentrate on school work
looks for any excuse to stay home from school
bored, unmotivated
withdraws from interacting with family and friends
uncharacteristically dependent or clingy
rarely smiles or laughs
more aggressive and tense than usual
increasingly selfish

overly sensitive to mild criticism
anxious and restless, unable to settle into constructive activity
craves food with sugar and salt
complains of headaches
has continual fears or nightmares
"locked" in front of the television
keeps feelings bottled up inside
prone to accidents
fatigued -- has an increased desire for sleep

The next step is to discover and respond to the causes underlying the children's feelings. Loss of a family member, divorce, abuse, and poverty are clearly the most harmful forms of stress for children. However, there are several new stressors facing children which are related to family, television, education, sports, and adult stress. They all encourage a "speeding up" of the childhood years, and treatment of children that, for many, is harmful to their growth. As I cover each type of stress, I will point out its major causes and symptoms, as well as strategies for helping children who suffer its effects.

## Family-Related Stress

Vance Packard, author of ***Our Endangered Children: Growing Up In a Changing World,*** has identified the spillover of parental stress onto children as a cause for concern. Many of today's parents are self-absorbed and detached from their children. They also experience a great deal of stress because of conflict with co-workers and supervisors. For example, Ann Crouter, a researcher from Penn State University, interviewed employed parents at the end of the work day and again two hours later at home. She found that problems with supervisors during the day led to arguments within the family that night. Research by Ellen Galinsky of Bank Street College found that for parents of young children (under 6 years old), 51% of the men and 68% of the women experienced a high degree of conflict between family and job responsibilities.

## *Causes and Symptoms*

For two-income families, the trend is to work long hours in order to keep up with the increasingly high cost of living. Robert and Rhona Rapoport, authors of ***Dual Career Families Re-examined,*** state that the strains of meeting the obligations of job and family are often too difficult for many working parents to handle. These families are especially vulnerable to the psychological strain of "mental overload" which occurs when the demands of home and occupation are excessive. Contrary to predictions 20 years ago that automation would result in a vastly reduced work week, the reality is that people are working more hours per week in order to keep up with their financial commitments.

While children whose parents work outside the home are more self-reliant because of increased responsibilities and independence, studies show that when parents work long hours, a price is paid. Surveys conducted by Ellen Galinsky and Judy David, authors of ***The Pre-School Years,*** identified the large number of hours parents work as having the most negative repercussions on home life, in the form of increased family tensions and health-related problems. Other studies by researchers Joseph Pleck and Halcey Bohen indicate that the greater the numbers of hours worked by mothers or fathers, the more likely there is to be family tension. The ***Fortune Magazine Childcare Study*** of 1987 found that the more hours on the job, the more likely the workers were to experience both stress and a greater sense that their job interferes with their family life.

Other studies have identified additional problems encountered by children whose parents are stressed. The ***General Mills American Family Report*** found that children express dissatisfaction with their parents for not giving them necessary attention. Urie Bronfenbrenner, author of the classic ***Two Worlds of Childhood: U.S. and U.S.S.R.***, explains that when children spend less time with parents, they are likely to spend more time with peers or watching television. The degree of interest in peer groups is influenced more by lack of attention and concern at home than by attraction to the group of friends. Children who become excessively peer-oriented and less family-oriented as they mature run the risk of engaging in more antisocial behaviors such as lying, teasing, and playing hooky.

It seems logical to conclude from these studies that if parents work less and spend more time with their children, both their and their children's stress will be reduced. However, this may not be a feasible option for many. There is also some disagreement about this among experts. Studies such as those completed by Adele and Allen Gottfried have concluded that it is the experiences to which children are exposed that are most important to their development, regardless of the employment situation of parents. Either way, providing an appropriate amount of time for parent-child interactions is clearly a critical factor in reducing children's stress.

Developmental psychologist David Elkind, writing in ***The Hurried Child***, believes that parents often seek to escape their own stress by pushing children to achieve early success in both school and sports. They may enroll their preschool children in programs emphasizing early academics, which often teach through formal instruction that is inappropriate for 3, 4, and 5 year-olds. They may also enter their primary grade children into highly competitive organized sports, which can be equally inappropriate. As will be shown in the following sections on sports-related stress and education-related stress, practices such as these push youngsters to do too much too soon, putting them at risk to develop apathy, anger, or negative feelings towards themselves.

Further, parents under stress often believe that their children are more precocious, mature, and sophisticated than children of previous generations. As a result, they treat their children as equals. Eventually, this leads to overly permissive parenting and a strong tendency to overindulge children by not setting or enforcing rules and limits. As Marie Winn states, "Children do not prosper when treated as equals."

It is natural for parents to want to evade the hassles of confronting inappropriate behavior from their children after a hard day's work, especially around dinner time. However, avoiding the responsibility to consistently define and enforce home rules is stressful to children. Children want and need the security of adult control, especially when they feel out of control. According to family therapist Dr. Sandra Rodman Mann, Assistant Professor of Parent Education at Fordham University, "Children often see this reluctance to set limits as evidence that their parents don't care enough to protect them."

## *Strategies for Helping Children Deal with Family Stress*

**Be a responsible parent.** Act with confidence in order to protect and guide children. This means finding a middle ground between authoritarian and permissive parenting. The goal is to provide children with high amounts of support (love, encouragement) and control (setting and supporting limits). Chapter 3 contains a discussion of ways to provide appropriate discipline.

**Schedule time to be with your children.** Allow for at-home time when you can focus directly on sharing with them. A good time for conversation is during a leisurely dinner. Plan activities ahead of time to engage in events that all family members will enjoy.

**Read the section in this chapter on Strategies for Reducing Stress in Adults' Lives.**

**Help fathers become more involved in the care of their children.** Studies have shown that men can be as nurturing, sensitive, and attuned to children as women. According to Nancy Chodorow from the University of California, a nurturing father encourages children both to achieve and to develop concern about people. Michael Lamb, author of ***The Role of the Father in Child Development,*** states that "the most influential fathers appear to be those who take their role seriously and interact with their children."

**Read to children every night.** Encourage children to choose books they would like to hear. When they show a strong interest in certain stories, ask them to recall and retell them. Avoid direct instruction in decoding words until children want to know what the words say. Then teach them by pointing to specific words as they are said.

**Seek organized sport activities that minimize "winning" and physical contact for children under 10.** Experts agree that competitive contact sports are inadvisable for young children. Even though your child may indicate a strong desire to participate, being a responsible parent entails providing protection. See the section in this chapter on Sports-Related Stress for an in-depth discussion of this issue.

**Seek out high-quality child care situations which contain language-rich environments and class sizes of 20 children or less.** Remember that because nearly 40% of all child care workers leave the profession every year, finding high-quality centers may be difficult. The National Association of Child Care Resource and Referral Agencies in Rochester, Minnesota provides a list of services available nationwide.

## Television-Related Stress

Recent research on children and the media makes it clear that most children watch an inordinate amount of television. There is evidence that infants begin paying attention to television at the age of 6 months. Preschoolers have been documented as watching 3 to 4 hours of television a day, while elementary-aged children view 15 to 25 hours a week. This amount of viewing can have a powerful and negative impact on their behavior.

### *Causes and Symptoms*

Excessive television viewing causes increased aggression, confusion and poor eating habits. Studies conducted by researchers Jerome and Dorothy Singer, well-known authorities on play and television, have consistently found that children who are heavy viewers of either aggressive action adventures or cartoons which show violence are more likely to exhibit aggressive behavior than youngsters who are not heavy viewers of such programs. Other researchers have found that aggressive preschoolers -- those who bite and kick -- are especially susceptible to the negative effects of viewing violence on television. In one study, these children were shown violent programs each day for a two-week period, which resulted in increased aggression in their play.

Aside from aggressiveness, children are often exposed to information and concepts on television that are beyond their ability to comprehend. Topics that have been considered unmentionable to children in the past, such as sexual promiscuity, rape, abortion, and homosexuality, are presented via television on a daily basis. Children become all too familiar with these adult "secrets" but cannot fully understand them until they develop the ability to think abstractly, which occurs anywhere from 12 to 18 years of age. As a result, they are confused, burdened, and stressed. In a sense, part of their childhood is taken away from them.

Television commercials have also been found to add to children's levels of stress. According to Betty Youngs, author of ***Stress in Children***, poor diets rank second only to emotional pressure as a source of stress, yet parents are pressured to buy "junk foods" by demanding children who have been influenced by commercials. And, to make matters worse, there are three times as many commercials aired during children's programs than during shows geared to adults.

Action for Children's Television, an organization which monitors TV's impact on youngsters, considers commercials -- with their emphasis on sugar-filled cereals, candy, and soda -- to be a greater problem than programs containing violence and sex. When children develop poor eating habits and do not receive the necessary nutrients, their bodies are incapable of dealing with stress and they become more vulnerable to health problems.

Another concern is that extensive television watchers fall behind their peers in intellectual development. A study completed by Roni Beth Tower and her colleagues suggests that because television is a passive activity, excessive viewing may alter children's ability for sustained attention and thought. The scenes in most shows change very quickly, encouraging the viewer to concentrate on a thought for only a brief period. Teachers nationwide have noted that students are impatient with long presentations, while an analysis of current textbooks, compared to those from 25 years ago, shows a dramatic decrease in the number of words used to transmit information and an increase in the use of illustrations and photographs.

### *Strategies for Helping Children Deal with Television-Related Stress*

**Use television less as a babysitter and more as a stimulator of family discussions.** This is the only way it can offer any real stress-reduction benefits to children. Viewing should be selective and occur with adults who explain what is happening in the show and to the characters. Point out positive character values such as honesty, loyalty, taking responsibility and showing respect for people and property.

**Place clear limits on the types of shows and the amount of time children are allowed to watch.** The American Academy of Pediatricians suggests a maximum of between one and two hours a day of TV viewing for all children. High quality video tapes, non-electronic games (board games, dramatic play), reading, and best of all, pretend play, are suggested forms of entertainment that are alternatives to television.

**Identify TV shows that stimulate pretend play.** Encourage children to make-believe they are the characters. Add props such as blocks and tinker toys to build walls and houses.

**Avoid shows that are scary, overwhelming, and difficult for young children to comprehend.** This includes news programs. It's best to limit news watching until children are in bed.

**Teach your children to be wise consumers.** Explain that the purpose of commercials is to persuade the viewer to purchase something. When children persist with requests for you to purchase what they see on TV, either say no and give a reason, or say, "I have to think about it." Take your time before making a decision.

**Join Action for Children's Television (ACT).** They are a lobbying group that supports legislation before Congress calling for greater regulation of children's programming. In the past, ACT has been effective in making programmers reduce television violence and advertisements for sugared foods.

**Call or write local TV stations and sponsors to support or criticize their shows.** Stations and advertisers do respond to feedback from the public.

## Education-Related Stress

As I discussed in the Introduction and Chapter 1, the push-down curriculum and further school "reforms" inspired by the ***Nation At Risk*** report have resulted in the teaching of young children through methods traditionally used with older students. These changes have resulted in major problems for children below the third grade: tension, boredom, and a negative attitude toward learning that can last throughout their school years.

## *Causes and Symptoms*

Carol Hoffman, early childhood supervisor for the Wilson, Pennsylvania public schools, and author of ***Curriculum Gone Astray: When Push Came To Shove,*** believes that it is a mistake to build curriculum from the twelfth grade down and not from kindergarten up. By the time curriculum planning reaches the primary grades, our objectives and goals for children are seriously out of sync with their developmental needs. She believes that "Today's curriculum, K-12, is developmentally inappropriate for today's students."

Nationally, the curriculum in grades kindergarten, one, and two has focused on teaching academics through excessive emphasis on paper and pencil activities. Teachers are teaching isolated skills in reading and math primarily through the use of worksheets and workbooks. While these methods and materials may be appropriate with older students, they are strikingly unstimulating to young children and fail to extend their thinking. There is little in the educational research literature which supports their use.

There has also been a "speeding up" of what is being taught to children. Acquisition of skills and concepts has been pushed downward. What used to be taught in the higher grades is now introduced in the lower grades. In regard to math, for example, most first grade children need opportunities to count, sort, and classify concrete materials. Instead, many first grade teachers have been required to teach math using abstract worksheets. They are also compelled to introduce concepts such as "whole number place value," even though many students have not mastered an understanding of counting and one-to-one correspondence.

This situation is causing an inordinate amount of stress on primary grade children. Dr. Irving Sigel, research scientist for the Educational Testing Service, says that "many children are having to exert enormous effort to succeed and thus are under considerable and continuing stress." Schools create tension when learning experiences are tedious, boring, and do not support developmental levels. Positive attitudes toward learning can be damaged when academic work is introduced too early. High rates of failure, which accompany an accelerated curriculum, make children feel incompetent and cause them to lose confidence in their ability to succeed in school.

## *Strategies for Helping Children Deal with Education-Related Stress*

**Promote the arts in your child's life.** If the school your child attends is excessively academic, provide opportunities for self- expression by seeking after-school and Saturday programs in art and music.

**Identify inviting learning materials which children can touch, manipulate, and wonder about.** Involve them in projects that motivate them to build, draw, read, and write about things that interest them.

**Encourage your school to follow the curriculum guidelines described in the book *Developmentally Appropriate Practice,* edited by Sue Bredekamp.** This is the best-selling guide to developmentally appropriate curriculum that the National Association for the Education of Young Children published in 1987, in order to help pre-schools and primary grades distinguish between appropriate and inappropriate teaching practices.

## Sports-Related Stress

All children need vigorous exercise and play activity on a regular basis. The preschool child enjoys sensorimotor (running, climbing, jumping) activities as well as imaginative play and games without rules. Primary grade children can be introduced to games with rules and organized sports if the focus is on teaching skills, building team spirit, and having fun. The danger for young children occurs when there is inadequate preparation and excessive competition or contact, because physical and/or emotional stress can result.

### *Causes and Symptoms*

Many primary school children spend most of their school days sitting, and they then spend their evenings watching television or playing video games. This lifestyle leaves them unprepared to start playing demanding sports, and makes them prone to injuries.

Surprisingly, the overall rate of sports injuries is highest for soccer and gymnastics. However, sports which create a high risk of collisions, such as football, may inflict the most severe physical harm on young children. This is due in part to the fact that muscles do not attain full volume and bones are not totally calcified until adolescence.

Physicians are recording more young children with adult-type sports injuries. An article in the ***Boston***

*Globe* reported that since 1985, the sports medicine clinic at Boston Children's Hospital has treated an average of 150 sports-injured youngsters per week. The number of child patients increased from 200 to 600 a month, and 90 percent of the children were hurt in organized events.

Many children suffer injuries to the "growth plates" located near their joints. A syndrome known as "little league shoulder," for example, can result from the repetitive trauma of throwing a baseball. Another example, called Osgood-Schlatter disease, is a knee-related syndrome frequently found in children who play soccer or baseball extensively.

Dr. Lyle Micheli, director of the Sports Medicine Division at Boston Children's Hospital, states "There is a whole new genre of injuries occurring in children engaged in organized sports, that rarely occurred in free play situations. These are the overuse injuries — the tendinitis of the shoulder, elbow, ankle, or hips; stress fractures often resulting from excessive training; and, in particular...stress syndrome of the knee." These overuse injuries tend to show correlations with particular sports. Knee problems often result from field sports such as football and soccer as well as long-distance running, while young gymnists may experience lumbar spine problems. Children who do excessive jumping and running may experience hip or hind foot problems.

Soccer appears to be particularly dangerous to children's eyes. Dr. Richard Kavner, Assistant Clinical Professor of Optometry at the State University of New York, notes that during the 1970s, eye injuries increased by 58 percent in all organized sports. In soccer, the fastest growing children's sport, the rate jumped 260 percent. One third of the eye injuries occurred in children between the ages of 5 and 14. Dr. Kavner highly recommends eye protection for children who participate in this sport.

The emotional impact of organized sports can also be severe, as too much emphasis on winning and losing tends to shake young children's self-esteem, because their self-esteem is closely tied to the outcome of a game. In a study called "Competitive Sports In The Elementary School," researchers Charles Jacobson and Michael Shaughnessy concluded that highly competitive sports are often harmful to both the physiological and psychological growth of young children. As stated in *National PTA 88*, many psychologists and teachers believe that children should not be placed in team sports that emphasize the importance of winning until age 10. When children feel pressured to win, the score becomes more important than learning fundamentals and playing fairly. Children begin to hope others fail, and may even help it happen, because it enhances their chance to win.

This inappropriate pressure at an early age may account for the high dropout rate from organized sports. A 1990 *NBC News/USA Today* study found that three out of four American children drop out of organized sports before the age of 15. Unfortunately, the adolescent years are precisely when engaging in organized competition is developmentally appropriate.

Terry Orlick and Cal Botterill, authors of *Every Kid Can Win*, write: "Research has established that when a child is still struggling to learn skills, the additional burden of being placed in front of an audience and being pitted against a rival is bound to have a negative effect on the child's performance and perhaps the child himself." Orlick recommends that children engage in cooperative games which support emotional development and encourage skills acquisition without fear of losing the game. His book, ***The Second Cooperative Sports and Games Book,*** contains many non-competitive activities for young children.

Play among 6, 7, and 8 year-olds works best when it is unstructured, rather than organized and directed by adults. The role of teachers and parents is to arrange equipment, play areas, and provide ideas, in order to enable children to initiate their own games, make and break their own rules, and determine the direction of the play.

In first and second grades, rules are an essential part of classroom learning. For example, there are phonics rules to remember and rules for adding two columns of numbers. Children need direct practice in creating and modifying their own rules in order to truly understand the concept of rules and the important role they play. This is one of the benefits of child-directed play provides.

When children participate in organized sports, it is best to keep in mind the advice of Ben Nelson, a school principal in Oxford, New York and nationally known speaker and consultant on youth and sports. He says "The goal is to have the children experience the joy of competition without the pressure to win." To accomplish this, parents and coaches need to de-emphasize the importance of winning, and pay attention to their children's skill progress and levels of personal enjoyment and satisfaction. This is especially true in contact sports.

## *Strategies for Helping Children Deal with Sports-Related Stress*

**Become more involved, not only in coaching, but in lobbying for more training of all coaches in recreational and town-sponsored organized sports.** The quality of adult leadership often determines the extent of children's learning. Similarly, the quality of adult coaching in organized sports is a key factor in teaching skills, promoting enjoyment, and reducing emotional and physical stress. Untrained coaches are likely to increase the intensity and duration of training, believing that "more is better" and "no pain, no gain." On the other hand, trained coaches understand children's limitations and know when an activity should come to an end.

**Obtain a pediatric assessment of a child's physical readiness for a given organized sport.** This includes: individual fitness or lack of it; evaluating the demands of the sport; and suggesting alternative fitness activities if the child cannot participate.

**Support a child's involvement in sports, but do not pressure him or her to join.** Allow the child to select the sport, but with your approval. Make a commitment to getting the children to practice and to the games.

**Look for stress signs resulting from the toll a particular sport is taking on a child.** Does the child appear to be having any fun? Is he continuously irritable about evaluations of his personal performance? Is there a tendency to take the blame for losses? Is she frequently injured or ill?

**Allow a child to quit if he or she appears to be "burned out."** Show that you are proud of their efforts in other areas. Interest may be reignited after time away and an increase in physical growth and ability.

**Set a good example during the games.** Adults who shout criticisms and correct the children, coaches, or officials from the sidelines make sports unpleasant for everyone.

## Implementing Strategies for Reducing Stress

Let me review the general procedures for preventing and reducing stress in children's lives. The first is to recognize stress when it occurs. The second is to discover the causes underlying the children's feelings and then take effective action. Two more elements in my strategy follow.

### *Use Pretend Play as An Outlet for Tensions*

Young children today have few opportunities to find natural relief from the daily stressors which confront them. Years ago, young children played outdoors with their friends after school and during the summer. They engaged in pretend play and took on powerful roles by planning, negotiating, creating rules and solving problems. Interestingly enough, these are the same skills which high school teachers say our children are currently lacking.

Pretend play is healthy for the development of young children, because they can ventilate pent-up frustrations while they learn many skills needed to succeed in the adult world. Marie Winn's description of today's children as "play deprived" refers to the unwholesome fact that few children in preschool and primary grades engage in enough pretend play. Instead of play-centered childhoods, children lead more adult-type lifestyles filled with purpose, achievement and competition. Outside of school, they are chauffeured from one organized activity to another. In their free time, when they are not involved in adult-directed learning experiences, they are usually watching television or playing video games. Winn believes that an excessive amount of TV watching and video game playing, combined with overly academic curriculums in the early grades, has discouraged imaginative play among 4 to 8 year-old children.

Video games heighten a child's interest in reacting instantaneously, emphasizing quick reflexes but in a limited number of ways. The excitement, challenges and frustrations this visual medium provides can serve as an escape from stresses in a child's life. However, children can become so addicted to this type of stimulation that they prefer it to the possibilities traditional play offers for working through their stress.

There are several traditional modes of play:

pretending (playing house)
constructing (building with blocks or legos, painting)
games with rules (checkers, marbles, monopoly)
gross-motor movements (tag)

All these modes involve children in social interactions, imagining, negotiating, exploring and experimenting. Studies have concluded that given an atmosphere of acceptance and active permission, children can use all these types of play to master common stress. Pretend play in particular allows children to take on roles and verbalize in situations in which anything is possible: dominoes can be dominoes at the same time as they represent members of a family. Pretend play prepares children to use symbols (words and numbers) in school and throughout life.

## *Create A Coping Plan*

The purpose of a coping plan is to provide an organized means of reducing stress through relaxation, and then eliminating stress through problem solving and action. This should be done for both the child and the adult involved. As noted in the section on family-related stress, children's stress may derive from the adults in their lives, so focusing solely on the child is not enough.

A list of strategies for helping children appears below. Each has been shown, through various studies, to be effective. The strategies consist of teaching ideas for the early childhood classroom, and parenting practices which can be implemented at home. Many of the strategies can be used in both locations. Information on reducing stress in adults' lives follow.

## *In The Classroom*

**Use "bibliotherapy" -- read stories to children that can help them recognize that others face the same stressors in their lives.** To locate literature with appropriate themes about young people's emotional problems, see Sharon Dreyer's ***The Bookfinder: A Guide To Children's Literature About The Needs and Problems of Youth Aged 2-15***, and ***Helping Children Cope: Mastering Stress Through Books and Stories*** by Joan Fassler. ***The Child In Crisis*** by Patricia Doyle and David Behrens provides advice for assisting children who are undergoing emotional turmoil. These references can be used by parents as well.

**Teach children how to relax their bodies at rest time or before activities that require concentration and attention.** Read ***Quiet Times: Relaxation Techniques for Early Childhood*** by Louise Binder Scott. The book contains stories, action rhymes, and quiet poems which have been tested and used successfully with preschool and primary grade students.

**Use quiet music to calm children before a reading lesson or after a gross-motor activity.** Try the record "Lullabies and Sweet Dreams," by Steve Halpern.

**Lead a visualization exercise while children are listening to soft music.** In a study titled "Stress Management Techniques for Young Children," nursery school director Francesca Piper concluded that visualization was "especially successful in calming and increasing the attention spans of members of the 4 and 5 year-old groups." Visualization can be done in small groups of ten or less. Pleasant images that are familiar to the children can be used, such as those found in favorite stories. Books that contain visualization activities are ***Flights of Fancy*** by Lorraine Plum and ***Spinning Inward*** by Maureen Murdock. Follow visualizations with art or building experiences.

**Be a play facilitator by setting the stage.** Use props, pictures and field trips to stimulate pretend play. Ask questions that acknowledge and extend the children's fantasy to motivate children, such as: "Do you need someone to take care of you?" or "Is that the doorbell?" Intervene gently during children's play to introduce concepts such as counting the steps out to the playground or counting the buttons on a sweater.

**Use role-playing to prepare a child for an upcoming, stressful event.** Rehearse the situation using other children as characters with predefined roles. Explore alternative ways to approach the situation. This is a good opportunity to teach children to be verbally clear about what they want and how they feel.

**Encourage children to take action by teaching individual and/or group problem solving:**

1) identify the problem that is causing stress in the child's life
2) list the possible solutions
3) select a solution and develop a plan
4) discuss the progress of the plan from time to time

The child or group should feel the plan provides control over the situation, in addition to taking care of specific problems.

**Allot time for each of the traditional types of play: pretending, constructing, games with rules, and gross motor movement games.** The NAEYC publication, ***Play: The Child Strives Toward Self-Realization,*** contains valuable information about teacher and parent interventions during play.

## *In The Home*

**Make a home assessment of what stress experts call the fitness triangle:**

1) nutrition and diet
2) physical activity and exercise
3) sleep and rest

Observe your child in relation to these areas and develop a plan to improve individual or family practices regarding one or more areas.

**Arrange a play area with toys and props that encourage children to act out their fantasies.** A tent can be made under a table, a large cardboard box can become a home or an office. Refer to ***Mr. Rogers' Play Book*** for ideas about toys and materials that can be used creatively.

**Join children in their fantasy play.** Take on a role and express imagination and playfulness.

**Use part or all of the following bedtime routines with your child.** Relax your child with a bath and a glass of warm milk. Read or tell a good story. For ideas, refer to *Creative Storytelling* by Jack McGuire. Turn out the lights, leaving on only the night light. Sit or lie next to your child. As you discuss the day's events, respond to the feelings you hear rather than take issue with the behavior. For example:

Child: "I got into a fight with Andrew today."
Parent: "You got angry at something he said or did?"
Child: "Yes, he's always picking on me and I couldn't take it anymore."
Parent: "You were pushed to your limit. Let's talk about ways to handle this without fighting."

After a few minutes of talk, ask your child to take three deep breaths, slowly taking in air through the nose and expelling it out of the mouth. Then, gently massage the neck and shoulder muscles while asking, "What is one thing you like about yourself?" After acknowledging the response, end the evening by saying, "One thing I really like about you is..."

For older primary children, try an alternative bedtime routine which reduces muscle tension. Dr.

Herbert Benson, in his book, ***The Relaxation Response***, first suggests asking your child to lie comfortably and to close his eyes. Then, ask him to breathe deeply but slowly. Have your child tense his feet for 5 seconds, then relax the muscles. Do the same with the ankles, legs, hips, fingers, wrists, arms, back, shoulders, buttocks, neck, jaw, face and eyes. Say: "Let go of the tension. Imagine it flowing out of your body like an ice cube melting in hot water." After all the muscles have been relaxed, sit quietly for a few minutes. Breathe normally for several minutes before getting up.

## Reducing Stress in Adults' Lives

Adult intervention in children's lives is vital to prevent or reduce stress. When teachers and parents help children develop coping strategies, children begin to feel they have more control over their own lives. However, in order to be most effective in helping children manage the events around them, adults need to cope with their own stress.

Certain conditions set the stage for stress. For example, Dr. Marion Hyson, in her article, "Playing With Kids All Day," reminds us that one source of stress for adults is the unpredictability of children and daily events. Children who appear to be content one minute may swing rapidly to anger and frustration. Tranquility may be suddenly pierced by an altercation or accident.

According to the ***Fortune Magazine Childcare Study***, breakdowns in childcare arrangements were significantly associated with higher levels of stress and stress-related symptoms. These include: shortness of breath, pounding or racing heart, back and neck pains, overeating, drinking more alcohol, smoking more, and taking more tranquilizers. The survey revealed that parents who had more worries about their children were more likely to have high levels of stress.

Another possible origin of stress is an irritating neighbor or colleague. Daily criticism and gossip from this person can have a demoralizing effect. Problems between spouses can be even more stressful, especially if they cannot be resolved quickly and effectively.

Financial pressures are often a source of stress at home and at work. Budget cuts may force a teacher to accept a larger class or a reduced amount of learning materials. A parent may have to take an additional job to pay for an unexpected repair bill.

Stress can also be self-generated. Parents and teachers who are achievement-oriented may place unrealistic demands on themselves. For instance, teachers may feel the need to create a continuous stream of creative projects, while parents may become overly involved with civic groups and committees.

What follows is a list of coping strategies for both teachers and parents, grouped into three action areas: understanding and managing your feelings, verbalizing your wants and needs, and educating yourself.

## *Understand and Manage Your Feelings*

Sometimes there is nothing one can do to change a problem situation except control one's own emotional reaction. Understanding the role of emotions is vital to managing your own stress, as well as helping children manage theirs. Learning to separate intellect and emotions from what appears to be an intolerable situation is an important skill. The following suggestions have been shown to be effective.

**Exercise.** When we exercise, blood leaves the brain and goes to the muscles. Feelings of anger, frustration, and anxiety are lessened. Exercise increases energy rather than depleting it. A walk around the block with the children, or even dancing with them, makes everyone feel better.

**Utilize relaxation techniques.** Breathing, meditation, biofeedback, yoga, and stretching techniques can be helpful.

**Develop or make time for personally meaningful interests or hobbies that allow for self-expression.** Hans Selye, author of ***The Stress of Life***, advises "Work hard in life at something you are good at. The aim of life is self-expression, an aim usually difficult to fulfill in our society." Thomas Armstrong's book, ***In Their Own Way***, recommends opportunities for expression through art, music, dramatic play, or physical movement in order to reduce stress.

**Participate in supportive discussion groups.** This is a safe way of expressing positive and negative feelings about children and your work. Locate formal or informal support groups.

**Do something helpful for someone else.** Not only does this feel good, it helps prevent wallowing in one's own concerns.

**Be honest with yourself as to why you continue in a stressful situation.** There is a price to pay for everything that is worthwhile. Are you paying the price for what you value?

## *Verbalize Your Wants and Needs*

It is important to be able to communicate feelings and thoughts when you feel a situation is unfair. For instance, teachers often feel conflicted when they are pressured to use inappropriate teaching materials that they philosophically disagree with. Or, a parent may resent the scanty help in household chores from a spouse and children. In both cases, it is important to maintain autonomy by verbalizing wants and needs.

**Rehearse assertive statements.** Communicate your thoughts and feelings to others: "I have a problem with the current situation. When...(describe situation), I feel... (describe feelings)... because...(give reasons for a change)."

**Make personal adjustments to the situation when verbalizations do not work.** For example, a teacher may find ways to adapt and vary certain educational materials without feeling a loss of personal control. Likewise, a parent may make her own decisions about what she will or will not tolerate. She can increase her sense of personal autonomy by delegating appropriate responsibilities to other family members, and by placing limits on the number of new responsibilities she accepts.

**Create change by rearranging the daily routine or by planning a trip.**

## *Educate Yourself*

Obtaining information is one way of lessening the uncertainty of stressful situations, because knowledge provides a basis for making appropriate decisions. For instance, children have a way of being predictably unpredictable. Teachers can reduce their stress by planning a curriculum and developing routines that create an atmosphere of predictability, yet allow for children's spontaneity. Parents can learn about child management techniques such as those described in Chapter 3.

**Obtain information about the developmental characteristics of a particular child or age group.** Information about a child's background, medical history, and stage of development may make a child's behavior more understandable, more predictable, and therefore, less stressful.

**Keep a written record of behavior problems in order to identify patterns.** Do problem behaviors tend to occur in the morning or afternoon? Before snack or after lunch? Once the pattern is clear, causes and solutions can often be identified. A child's progress is also more easily recognized when reviewing written records. For example, a child may still be difficult to control in March, but behavior actually improved because he or she was biting others in February.

**Start a reading or viewing program.** Identify books, magazines, and videos that will give you new thoughts, energy, and outlooks.

Discipline issues often create a great deal of stress for teachers, parents and children alike. Chapter 3 explains how to build a foundation for successful relationships.

*Practice* 3

# Create respect for adult leadership

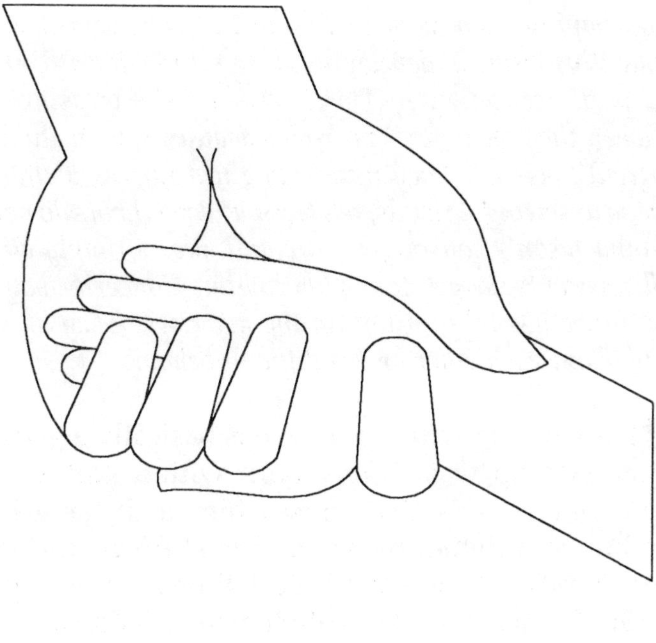

*Jason is a bright 4 year-old child, raised by patient and loving parents. But Jason is not a happy child. He often tests the limits set by his parents, resisting reasonable requests to go to bed or leave the playground. At those moments, Jason is likely to "dig in" and oppose any attempt to stop what he is involved in, resulting in scenes of anger, frustration, and tears. He does the same thing in nursery school and with his baby sitters. What does the future hold for a child who seems to be at war with his parents, his teachers and other children?*

*Jason's parents are bewildered by his uncooperative behavior at such an early age. Because they are gentle people who want a peaceful home, they generally give in to his demands, hoping his behavior will improve as he gets older. Consequently, Jason is developing a disrespect toward his parents as authority figures. They, in turn, feel increasingly guilty when they see other 4 year-olds acquiesce so easily to their parent's wishes. They never imagined raising a child could be so upsetting. Friends, relatives, and neighbors do not understand Jason's contrary nature and have strongly advised his parents to get tough with him. Concern about Jason's future has taken a toll on the marriage. They have begun to blame each other for his difficult behavior.*

What's wrong with Jason? He is basically a good child who was simply born with a "difficult temperament" -- one that causes him to behave in demanding and defiant ways. In ***The Difficult Child,*** Stanley Turecki, Assistant Clinical Professor of Psychiatry at Mount Sinai School of Medicine, defines temperament as the natural, inborn style of behavior. It is a child's set of inherited dispositions and behaviors, used to express satisfaction or displeasure with the world. According to Turecki, who founded the Beth Israel Difficult Child Program in New York, approximately 15 percent of all children are born with difficult temperaments. This means between two and three million young children in the United States fall into this category. While they are not "average," they are still "normal."

Abnormality implies the presence of a clear, diagnosable disorder. "Temperamentally difficult" children are simply different. Difficult children can be unpredictably hot-tempered at times, and they are generally demanding and uncooperative. They are not deliberately cruel, but they have little desire to please others. They get upset and angry when their needs are not responded to immediately. The temperamentally difficult child is often in a negative mood, reacts intensely to change, and is irregular in sleep and feeding habits.

Some children are born with "easy" temperaments. As infants, they smile much of the time and sleep through the night. As they get older, they are generally cooperative and seek to create family harmony. They care about what adults think of them and seem to delight in finding ways to make adults happy. The temperamentally easy child smiles at strangers, approaches new situations with a positive attitude, and reacts mildly to changes.

Other children are born predisposed toward shyness -- what researchers describe as "slow-to-warm-up" behavior. When someone comes to visit and tries to talk to a temperamentally shy child, the child usually pulls away. This slow-to-warm-up child responds mildly to change and quietly withdraws from new situations.

The categorization of children according to temperament is based on the pioneering New York Longitudinal Study (NYLS) conducted by Alexander Thomas and Stella Chess, Professors of Psychiatry at New York University. The study, begun in 1956, is described in their book, ***Know Your Child***.

The temperaments of 133 infants were identified at birth. Sixty-five percent fit clearly into one of the three categories. Thirty-five percent of the children showed moderate combinations of temperamental traits that did not neatly fall into one particular category. All these children and their parents were followed for the next 30 years. The primary objective was to determine if their individual temperaments influenced psychological development, in either healthy or unhealthy directions.

The NYLS identified nine specific temperamental traits:

1) **Adaptability** (Can the child deal with change and transitions?);
2) **Regularity** (Is the child hungry or sleepy at the usual times?);
3) **Approach/Withdrawal** (What is the response to new places, people, and food?);
4) **Mood** (Does the child tend to react positively or negatively?);
5) **Intensity** (How loud is the child, usually?);
6) **Activity level** (Is the child calm or in constant motion?);
7) **Distractibility** (Can the child pay attention or is he or she distracted easily?);
8) **Sensory threshold** (What is the child's reaction to texture of foods and clothes, smells, lights, and colors?);
9) **Persistence** (Does the child persist with an activity? Is there a stubborn reaction to parental requests?)

Chess and Thomas arrived at some very interesting conclusions. They found that the first five traits were specific to children identified as possessing difficult temperaments. That is, these children were poorly adaptable, irregular, had trouble with new situations, were usually in a negative mood, and had high intensity. No striking differences between boys and girls were found. In all instances but higher activity for boys, the sex differences were scattered and, in general, inconsistent. Thomas and Chess also found that it is not uncommon for temperamentally easy or shy children to possess one or two difficult characteristics.

The New York Longitudinal Study concluded that there is a biologically determined pattern of temperament in newborns which tends to persist and dominate in the early years. However, interactions with parents and others may intensify or modify original temperaments. As children grow older, environmental influences such parental treatment, peer groups and school experiences take on more importance in shaping behavior. While the effect of temperament in adulthood varies with individuals, it generally becomes less of a factor with age. The NYLS conclusion -- that temperamental traits, though inborn, can be modified -- has been confirmed by research studies both in the United States and in Europe.

In 1987, James Dobson, psychologist and former Associate Clinical Professor of Pediatrics at the University of Southern California, completed an extensive investigation of 37,000 children. As described in his book, ***Parenting Isn't for Cowards***, Dobson collected and summarized information about temperamentally strong-willed (difficult) children from 35,000 parents. He found that twice as many children were identified as strong-willed, compared with those labeled compliant (easy). Dobson concluded that while temperamentally difficult children are stressful to raise, these children can turn out quite well if parental leadership is established in the early years. It is often comforting to parents of difficult children to know that children's futures are not fixed at the age of 6. Dobson found that 85 percent of strong-willed children accepted parental values and beliefs by the time they reached young adulthood.

There is less unanimity among researchers as to how difficult children do in school. Whereas Chess and Thomas found high achievement scores and high IQ to be more closely related to youngsters with difficult temperaments, Dobson's study concluded that it was the compliant children who received better grades overall at all levels of schooling, had more friends, and tended to have higher self-esteem, compared to strong-willed youngsters. Strong-willed children did not do as well in school, according to Dobson, because of their tendency to challenge authority and their forceful desire to have their own way. And even though they had fewer friends, they were more peer-dependent.

This latter finding is surprising because years ago, Dobson predicted that strong-willed children would be more likely to say "no" to negative actions of a peer group. His study, however, showed that in many cases this gravitation toward the peer group caused strong-willed youngsters more problems.

## The Importance of Respect for Parental Leadership

In *The Strong-Willed Child,* Dobson states that "developing respect for parents is the critical factor in child management," because a child's attitude towards others is based upon the parent-child relationship. As in other areas of development, children pass through a series of stages in regard to respect. Respect for parents leads to "mutual respect" between children and their peers and teachers. Mutual respect then leads to self-respect.

Before they turn 7, children need to acquire a healthy respect for their parent's ability to define and enforce household rules with consistency and fairness. Children who are able to follow parental leadership in the early years demonstrate better overall self-control and are more likely to form positive relationships throughout childhood, leading to self-respect during the teenage years. As with all developmental processes, success in one stage depends on achieving the goals of the preceding stage.

Respect for adult authority can only be achieved when children are treated with strength and confidence, combined with sincere affection and concern. When parents and teachers continually accept behaviors which exceed the boundaries they have identified, children lose respect for adult leadership ability.

In homes where parents maintain the leadership role, the family is usually much happier. As reported in the book *No Single Thread*, a study conducted by a group of psychiatrists led by Dr. Jerry Lewis found that in healthy families, leadership and power are clearly held by the parents. Children's expressed opinions are considered and high levels of autonomy are encouraged, but the ultimate power remains with the parents.

Dr. Lewis also found that negotiation is common in healthy families. Negotiation assists open communication, works well, and can be used frequently once children respect and accept parental authority and leadership. The opportunities for negotiation continue to increase as children get older, more mature, and are able to think more logically. However, with young children, certain routines such as bedtime, attending religious services, and completing homework should not be negotiated.

I have observed that too often negotiating with young children becomes translated into allowing them to satisfy their own desires at the expense of other family members. When parents need cooperation, but instead are met with resistance, they need to act confidently rather than "back off" and allow the children to be in control. Parents have the authority and the responsibility to make reasonable requests that are in the best interests of their children. Cooperating with these requests is how children learn to gain respect for parent and teacher leadership.

Selma Fraiberg, former Professor of Child Psychoanalysis at the University of Michigan Medical School, supports the importance of early parental management. In her classic book, ***The Magic Years***, she urges parents to help their children control their negative impulses as early as 18 months of age. She writes that "...patterns of parental control which are established in the earliest years of life serve as the patterns for self-control in later years..." At ages 2, 3 and 4, children do not possess the internal motivation to be good. Parents need to provide that motivation, so that a conscience, which emerges by age 5 or 6 and is largely developedthrough parental teachings, can restrain certain behaviors viewed as disrespectful. By age 9 or 10, the conscience becomes a stable part of the personality.

## *The Pitfall of Over-Permissiveness*

The demanding behavior of children can intensify when parenting or teaching practices are overly permissive, because responses to children's demands can either aggravate or diminish potential problems. Saying "I give up" to a child, especially if he or she walks the other way when called, does little to encourage more cooperative behavior. Making empty threats, or remarks like "You're driving me crazy," will erode any inclination to develop respect for adult authority when the child's demands are unreasonable.

Experts have noted that since the late 1960s, there has been a shift toward overindulging children by not setting or enforcing rules and limits. In a 1974 article, Dr. Benjamin Spock wrote that the "inability to be firm is, to my mind, the commonest problem of parents in America today. Parental firmness makes for a happier child." Dr. Spock's statement is just as true now. Nationally, preschool directors and teachers complain about the number of children who lack self-control because their parents find it almost impossible to say "no" to anything.

Overly permissive adults tend to:

be undemanding of children
have inconsistent rules or no rules
have low standards and expectations for children
assume children are their friends and equals

Children of overly permissive parents tend to:

develop emotional or behavioral problems due to inadequate guidance
feel neglected and confused
resent parent's attempts to be too friendly

Many of today's parents were greatly influenced by the social upheavals of the 1960s and the changing attitudes of the 1970s. Slogans of the time, such as "Do your own thing," called into question the role of authority. Today, a large number of parents are reluctant to tell their children what to do. They are more comfortable treating children as equals and believe that keeping them happy will discourage them from disobedience.

Dorothy Corkille Briggs writes in her book, ***Your Child's Self-Esteem***, "When a child feels valued and loved, he wants to cooperate; he is more interested in negotiating conflicts." While this statement is generally true, the role of inborn, difficult temperamental traits is not mentioned. Children with high energy and intensity, poor adaptability, or negative moods, are not likely to be interested in cooperating with parents. Everyone agrees that the communication of love is important, but it must be combinedwith the ability to guide behavior.

Children born with difficult temperaments and raised in a heavily materialistic world present a special dilemma. Their demanding and stubborn behavior, along with their desire for immediate external fulfillment, is a volatile combination that can anger, frustrate, and fatigue the most caring adults. In families where parents do not assume a leadership role, children have an inordinate amount of power in family decisions and can make everyone miserable, including themselves. They do what they want to do when they want to do it, regardless of their parent's wishes, but they are not yet mature enough to make wise decisions about their own best interests.

Affluent parents who are overly permissive with their children encourage what psychologist Dan Kiley calls the "Peter Pan Syndrome." This occurs when every whim is catered to, and children then become interested only in fun things that are easy to do. They also quickly grow angry when parents do not meet their demands for material things. As I pointed out in the discussion of television-related stress, children are bombarded with highly sophisticated advertisements designed to stimulate purchases of toys, clothes and candy. When parents indulge the resulting demands in an effort to keep children happy, they reward the children's behavior and make it more likely to reoccur.

Separate studies by Eleanor Macoby and Dan Olweus have found that when parents reduce pressures against aggressive and impulsive behavior, hard-to-manage children become even more difficult to control. What is best for young, temperamentally difficult children is not to treat them as equals and attempt to reason and negotiate every decision, but to take firm stands on important issues while remaining sensitive to the children's feelings and need for self-esteem.

## *Developing a Good Fit*

Chess and Thomas recommend that parents develop a "good fit" between their expectations and children's temperaments and abilities. They found that when relationships between parents and children were smooth, it was because of a good fit. This occurs when parents encourage children's efforts, appreciating and applauding their attempts to meet their own goals. This may entail significant adaptation and flexibility on the part of the parent, if the parent's personality and expectations clashes with the child's temperament. With temperamentally easy children, a good fit occurs naturally because these children are so interested in pleasing others. The quality of interaction with these children is usually positive.

A good fit between a parent and a shy child occurs when the parent takes the child's basic nature into account and gently encourages social interactions. Parents need to teach shy children social skills in unpressured ways. According to Phillip Zimbardo, author of ***The Shy Child***, shyness predisposes children to be extremely concerned about others' social evaluation of them. They desperately want to be accepted by other children, but unlike the easy child, do not know how to accomplish this. Parents and teachers can help enormously once they realize that a shy child is so sensitive to rejection, he or she is likely to avoid people and situations that have the potential for criticism. It is not enough to tell children to be "nice" to each other. Refer to the section on social development in Chapter 1 for specific strategies to use with a temperamentally shy child.

Children with difficult temperaments often provoke parents into responding negatively, causing a "poor fit." It is, however, possible to change a poor fit into a good fit. Take the case of Nancy, one of the subjects in the NYLS who was identified as possessing a difficult temperament from birth. Her father was critical and punitive, because he could not accept her intense and negative reactions to changes and to new situations. It seemed that Nancy's way of responding was always the opposite of what he expected. He wanted her to become easy-going, quiet, and able to adapt quickly to new situations. However, these were impossible expectations for Nancy to meet.

With such a "poor fit" between Nancy and her father, she began to have explosive outbursts by the age of 6. She was also afraid of the dark, sucked her thumb, and had trouble making friends. The father saw no reason why he should change. To him, Nancy was "just a rotten kid." However, when Nancy reached the fourth and fifth grades, she showed evidence of musical and dramatic talent. Her father, with some guidance, was able to change his behavior and begin to praise, support, and encourage his daughter in areas he considered desirable. In other words, a much better "fit" resulted, in part because of Nancy's increased achievements and maturation, but primarily because her father was able to respond more positively to her. Now in her late twenties, Nancy is a poised, self-confident adult with clear goals that she is successfully pursuing.

Nancy's case illustrates three NYLS conclusions that all parents of temperamentally difficult children should keep in mind:

1) children's futures are not fixed at the age of 6,
2) parental change can do much to modify and shape behavior,
3) environmental influences, such as school experiences and the attitude of peer groups, take on more importance as children grow older.

## *Parenting Styles*

In a study parallel to the NYLS and reported in 1971, Diana Baumrind of the University of California found a definitive relationship between parental attitude and the child's pattern of behavior. She described three types of parenting styles: **permissive, authoritarian** and **authoritative.** A **permissive** style allows a child maximum freedom but contributes little to children's sense of security. With an **authoritarian** style, parents demand obedience in such a way that children's independence is severely restricted, at the same time that they may be deprived of love and affection. The **authoritative** style provides love and caring balanced with firm and consistent guidance. It is characterized by substantial amounts of support (encouraging, praising, listening) simultaneous with substantial amounts of control (setting clear limits and reasonable consequences).

For the shy child, who needs to be brought out, the authoritative style is most likely to create a feeling of confidence and security. Authoritative parents touch and talk to their children very frequently, and show unconditional, no-strings-attached love. The authoritarian style, on the other hand, increases the shy behavior. It demands good behavior while withholding affection, which frightens these children and makes them withdraw even more. Permissive parenting also does little to make the shy child, who tends to have more nightmares and sleeping disorders, feel protected.

## Managing Difficult Children

What does the future hold for difficult children who seem to be at war with parents and others? Baumrind did not consider the effect that changing parental style would have on children's behavior. However, Turecki, Thomas, Chess, and Dobson all did, and they agree that when parents of temperamentally difficult children received some guidance, the children became more cooperative. Conversely, temperamentally difficult children who are poorly managed by their parents are at greater risk for having dissatisfying, tense relationships with both adults and peers. A parent who had read every book she could find about temperamentally difficult children, and whose own child had reached the age of 20, tells an encouraging story: "At first, we went through a fumbling stage. We were overly permissive and rationalized our son's difficult behavior. But our diligence and hard work has paid off. His strong independence, high energy level, and yes, stubbornness, have been channeled into constructive directions. The traits that made us crazy when he was younger, now breathe life into him."

Dr. Turecki is generally optimistic about the future of temperamentally difficult children. He states that the very traits that cause problems in childhood, if handled properly, can result in characteristics in young adulthood that are viewed as assets. For example, high-activity children may eventually do well in competitive careers. A negative mood can be an asset in naturally serious professions such as law and medicine.

However good the prognosis for temperamentally difficult children, the happy ending seems very unlikely to parents new to this type of child. Because children are reflections of their own skill and status, parents want their children to behave in ways that will bring positive comments from others. Difficult children generate the opposite response. Lecturing to so many parent audiences has made me painfully aware of the degree to which parents of difficult children suffer guilt and isolation. They often think they are only ones with such problems, and that their inadequate parenting is what caused the extreme behaviors.

Becoming aware of temperamental predisposition and implementing strategies for handling it reduces parental anxiety. The information helps parents adopt more positive behavior patterns and make better decisions. They also realize that the predisposition cuts across stereotypes. Often, after one of my lectures, a parent will stand up and tell about the "horrendous" behavior of a 7 or 8 year-old — answering back, refusing to cooperate, extreme jealousy, verbal taunting of a younger sibling (negative behaviors are invariably intensified upon the birth of a new child). I turn to the audience and ask whether it is a boy or a girl that the parent is talking about. The audience invariably says it's a boy. To their surprise, the parent often says "No, it's my daughter." In my own experience, like that of the NYLS, there have been as many descriptions of temperamentally difficult girls as boys. The only thing that is consistent is the parents' frustration.

Turecki studied parents of temperamentally difficult children and found them to be under stress. Out of 149 families with such children, 89 percent of the mothers said they were not coping, 69 percent reported strains in the marriage, and 92 percent said their discipline style was ineffective. Difficult children's predisposition to place their needs ahead of anyone else's makes raising and teaching them a formidable task, even when handled with skill and dedication.

It is not easy for parents and teachers to remain calm when their authority is challenged. For parents especially, the potential for anger is ever present. When adults are angered by children who reject their leadership, threats and yelling typically result. In fact, I have been told by the best and most dedicated parents about occasional episodes of rage where they had to physically remove themselves from the child's presence in order to regain control. Anger does little to manage the temperament of a difficult child, or to motivate him or her to change. It is ironic that temperamentally difficult children appear happier when limits on their behavior are enforced in a calm and consistent manner. They feel secure and comforted when they realize the adults are in charge and in control.

To create respect for their leadership, parents of temperamentally difficult children need to combine an abundance of love with confident discipline. Temperamentally difficult children, like all children, need to be shown they are valued and important. They need warmth and affection to help them feel secure. Setting firm limits without building close relationships causes adults and children to become adversaries. Relationships devoid of affection can deteriorate quickly with harmful consequences to the child.

Both parents and teachers need a plan of action that will guide them in responding to resistant behavior with conviction and confidence. Problems often result when there is not a plan to implement clear and practical strategies. The strategies that follow are a synthesis of ideas presented by the authors previously discussed in this chapter, along with my own experiences as a parent and teacher.

## *Strategies to Create Respect for Parent & Teacher Leadership*

Although parents of temperamentally difficult children have the most overt problems with discipline, all parents and teachers come across situations where their will seems to be in conflict with their children's. A one-sided approach that emphasizes "getting tough" or "cracking down" may seem helpful in the beginning, but in the long term it is an ineffective way to build respect. The overall strategy in disciplining is to help the child gain self-control, while at the same time keeping the child's self-esteem intact. This is accomplished by communicating a caring attitude and concurrently enforcing firm limits on disrespectful and otherwise inappropriate behavior.

It also is important to remember that adult leadership involves more than disciplining. It encompasses teaching and helping each child realize his or her full potential. The absence of overt discipline problems with temperamentally shy and easy children can be deceiving. There are often hidden problems which require sensitivity. Although the easy child functions in a sociocentric manner, recognizing the needs of others as a matter of course, he or she may occasionally rebel. Often the cause is that a difficult sibling or classmate gets more of the goodies and the adult attention. Without indulging the inappropriate behavior, parents need to use such incidents as a signal that they need to adapt their own behavior to better meet the easy child's needs. Shy children's problems are generally hidden because of their overwhelming need to please. However, it is not uncommon to see an expression of fear on their faces. Again, this should be a signal to parents or teachers to intervene for the child's welfare.

**Privately identify children as temperamentally easy, shy, or difficult, but do not use the label publicly.** Using such labels in front of the child or others can become a self-fulfilling prophecy which lasts for many years. "Sticks and stones may break my bones, but labels last forever."

**Accept the child's basic temperament and style of responding to the world.** Be sympathetic to the temperamentally shy or difficult child. The combination of love with limits or other interventions communicates an understanding that their behavior is not totally under their control. They need your help in managing their inborn temperament.

**Consider teaching assertiveness skills to temperamentally easy children.** These children, who are so geared to making others happy may forget themselves. Coach them by telling them it's desirable to communicate their wants and needs to others through "I" messages, such as "I don't like it when you leave me out of the game," or "I want to play, too." Read the book ***Parent Effectiveness Training*** by Thomas Gordon for more information on "I" messages.

**With shy children, use an authoritative style that emphasizes supportive and caring behaviors.** Since these children are more emotionally fragile, enforce rules firmly but gently. Be sure to hug them a lot, listen carefully, and demonstrate unconditional love.

**When a child is showing disrespect, evaluate the child's conduct by identifying one behavior at a time which is of greatest concern to you.** For example, is the child answering back in a rude or sarcastic manner? Is he refusing to respond to a reasonable request? Is she acting in an uncooperative and self-centered manner, intentionally breaking things or displaying bad temper tantrums?

**Determine where the behavior is coming from.** When the negative behavior is the result of inborn temperament, it is important to be sympathetic toward the child. Teach the child about her temperament (without labeling it) rather than being critical. Empathic statements are especially helpful in this regard. For example, the child who has been prepared for an upcoming change of schedule but is "poorly adaptable," may refuse to cooperate. An empathic response would be: "I know it's hard for you to stop doing something you really enjoy, but I'd like you to put the materials away so we can go outside." To the high activity/high intensity child, an empathetic comment would be: "I know it's difficult to calm down, but I'd like you to sit for a few minutes and rest." A response to a child in a negative mood might be: "I know you're not in a good mood right now. Is there anything I can do to help you?"

**Ask yourself whether you're taking a child's behavior too personally.** Remember that the temperamentally difficult child is not consciously planning and scheming to make your life miserable. Dr. Turecki advises that anytime you say to yourself, "Why is he doing this to me?", you are too involved and on the wrong track. It's more accurate and calming to view the behavior as normal and difficult for the child to control.

**Determine whether the behavior stems from natural carelessness and irresponsibility, which are a part of childhood.** Forgetting, dawdling, procrastinating, and knocking things over are typical childlike behaviors. Childhood foolishness and inconsistency are nature's way of insulating children from the pressures and responsibilities of life. With patient teaching and guidance, however, children gradually develop personal responsibility. If the child continues to be careless and irresponsible, it may be necessary to have him gently experience the natural consequences of the acts. For instance, continuously forgetting to put one's toys back where they belong may mean that he will not be allowed to play with them for a short period of time. Similarly, continued dawdling may cause a child to miss her favorite activity.

**Prepare temperamentally difficult children for changes of schedule.** Over and over again after my lectures, parents describe their embarrassment in front of relatives and friends regarding the unpredictable behavior of their difficult children. One mother summed it up when she said to a very large group, "My child just doesn't show well." My advice to these parents is not to take anything for granted. Prepare the child before you step out of the house. Let them know what to expect. Tell them where you're going and how you expect them to respond. "I want you to say hello to everyone. Grandma likes it when you help her in the kitchen. There are no toys there, so let's bring some." Preparation is one key to success. Another is emphasizing what the child should do, rather than stressing what not to do.

**Keep a written record of significant daily behaviors.** Since positive change evolves slowly, a diary can be helpful in determining and celebrating progress. It is not unusual for children to improve dramatically and then temporarily revert back to old patterns of behavior, especially when under stress.

**Clearly identify rules and the consequences for breaking them.** A child needs to know precisely what is expected of him at home or in school. Forbidden behaviors should be stated clearly and simply. It is best to follow any rule violation with a reminder and then a consequence that is brief and fair. Know beforehand what consequences you will impose when a child deliberately disregards a known rule, putting your authority to the test. A temperamentally difficult child will be more inclined to cooperate if he or she knows that a reasonable, but negative consequence will immediately follow when a rule is broken. An example would be a brief separation from peers or parents. A youngster who answers an adult back in a disrespectful manner may be isolated for a few minutes. In school, the child can be seated in a chair separated from the other children. At home, the child can be sent to his or her room. The time of separation should be related to the child's age. A 4 year-old is isolated for four minutes, and a 6 year-old for six minutes. Sending a 4 year-old to her room for 45 minutes is ineffective, because it is excessive and may create resentment within the child.

**Also use the withdrawal of a privilege as a consequence.** This technique works when it is closely related to the inappropriate behavior and implemented immediately after an occurrence. For example, continual fighting with a friend may mean that the children are forbidden to play with each other for one day. Materials left on the floor can result in a child not being allowed to play with them for one day. For young children, "punishment" should be brief and to the point, not a prolonged prison sentence.

**Maintain a united front between parents.** In a two-parent home, both parents need to discuss how they will handle situations, and when possible, come to an agreement about the type of action to take prior to an incident. They may disagree in private, but in front of the child it is important that they agree. To do otherwise will encourage the child to be manipulative and pit parent against parent.

**Take action in a predetermined, calm manner.** Use the "Toughlove Motto": "Say what you mean, mean what you say, and do what you say you are going to do!" Once the inappropriate behavior has been targeted and the consequence identified, it is time to act when the child puts the adult's authority to the test. Rehearse a quick, confident, and calm response to the difficult behavior. For example, a disrespectful answer such as "I don't care what you think!" may be followed by the adult simply stating, "I will not allow you to speak that way to me," and quickly imposing a consequence involving isolation or withdrawal of privilege.

**Follow-up negative consequence with reassurance.** Shortly after the negative consequence has been completed, it is especially important that the adult meet with the child to give reassurance that he or she is still a worthy child who is cared about. At that time, the teacher or parent can acknowledge the child's positive traits and express faith that future behavior will improve. The parent can communicate love, discuss what occurred and why, and use the situation to teach valuable lessons. This is an especially good time to discuss how to verbalize feelings when angry or upset, instead of attacking the adult or another child. Suggest and guide the child to rehearse statements such as "I'm not happy right now," as an alternative to "Leave me alone!"

**Make rules clear and visible in school.** The instances of difficult behavior are more likely to decrease if the curriculum is stimulating and materials-based. Bored students are more apt to be disruptive than those who are involved. To help students understand what is acceptable or unacceptable behavior, teachers can post and discuss charts that pictorially display or state classroom rules and related consequences. Positive consequences, such as special games and social times, are earned when the rules are followed. The goal is always to manage temperamental traits while simultaneously helping children develop self-esteem.

**Avoid developmentally inappropriate consequences such as writing students' names on a chalkboard and keeping them after school.** These practices are inappropriate for young children because they are a source of embarrassment and create negative attitudes toward school. Prolonged punishment may also discourage initiative in children who grow overly concerned about doing anything wrong.

**Continually assess your own behavior.** The power of the adult as a role model for teaching children important behaviors can hardly be overstated. Children watch parents and teachers and imitate what they do much more than what they say. As adults, we need to express appreciation, demonstrate honesty, and show compassion for others if we want to increase those behaviors in children.

**Make a conscious effort to stay calm and focused.** With temperamentally difficult children, parents will typically get involved in power struggles, yell, threaten or spank, and get dragged down to the level of the child. These behaviors, however, are ineffective and can be detrimental to the development of a child's self-esteem. Teachers are usually less emotional about individual children since they may have 25 or more students in a class. Yet, temperamentally difficult youngsters are a real challenge and can disturb the composure of the most knowledgeable educators, often forcing them to bristle and lose their poise. Periodically use the following questions to evaluate your ability to model positive behaviors and develop good rapport with children.

Do I demonstrate and discuss the values I believe in and want children to imitate, such as respect, honesty, compassion, creativity, responsibility and the importance of hard work?

Do I encourage children to develop an appropriate sense of humor? Am I capable of using humor to develop closer relationships, defuse tension, or improve a child's mood?

Do I discuss the positive things the children have done? Do I "catch them" being good by regularly recognizing their efforts with sincere praise?

Do I avoid comparing children to their siblings or their friends? Do I understand that the basis for most feelings of inferiority is comparison? How did I feel as a child when compared with others?

To what extent do I value listening to children? Do I give them my undivided attention when they want to talk to me? Do I show them I am sincerely interested?

Do I allow for time to be spent individually with children?

These strategies lay the foundation for children starting life and proceeding through childhood with trust in adult leadership. In Chapter 4, I discuss what parents and teachers should know in order to protect children from school failure.

*Practice* 4

# Protect children from school failure at the beginning

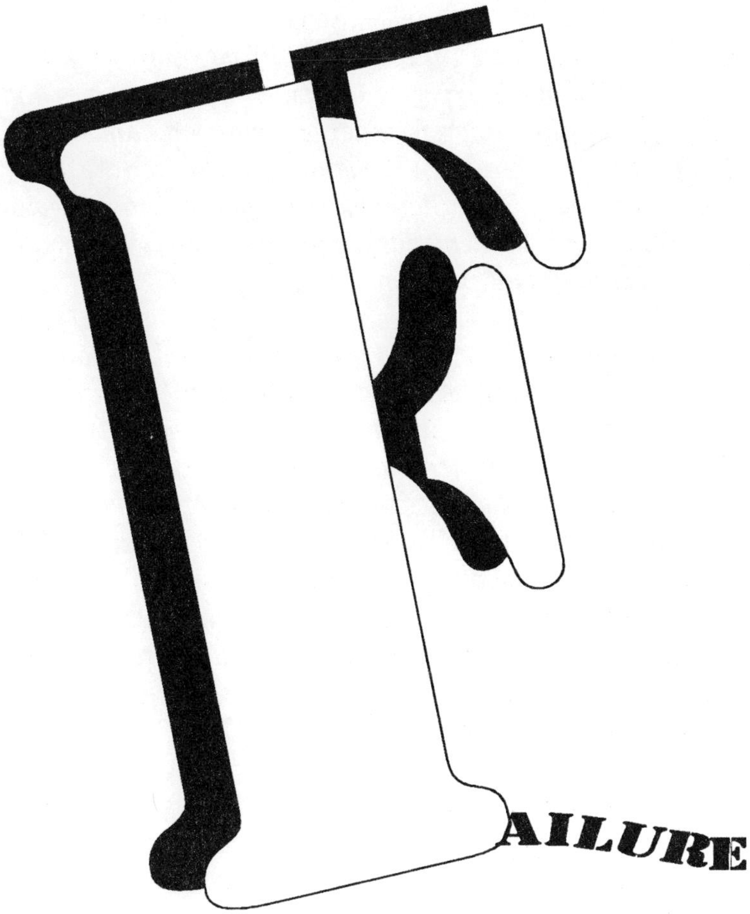

*Mrs. Bohme is an experienced, dedicated kindergarten teacher who is under a great deal of pressure. Years ago, her classroom was filled with stimulating materials and active learning experiences, which could be matched to each child's level of ability and skill development. The children were unhurried and allowed to learn new skills when they were ready, without fear of judgment. But by the mid-1980s, her district's school administrators were under increasing pressure to improve all students' achievement scores. This forced a change in Mrs. Bohme's style and methods of teaching.*

*The learning centers, blocks, and art easels have been replaced with worksheets and a teacher-directed reading program. The children are grouped by ability for reading instruction. Mrs. Bohme is expected to "cover" specific topics and learning objectives to prepare her students for standardized achievement tests. As a result, many of the children are under considerable stress. They don't have the maturity to cope with one or another of the demands of the curriculum. Kindergarten is a very difficult place for them.*

*Timothy, for example, is very knowledgeable about the world around him but has difficulty sitting still and complying with directions. He is constantly in motion and easily distracted. Melissa is nervous and fearful much of the time. She lacks confidence and is frustrated with tasks that require her to work independently. Matthew's speech is difficult to understand and he shows little interest in books. Almost one-third of the children in the class demonstrate behaviors similar to these three students. Many of them are "summer children," who just turned 5 during the summer months before entering kindergarten.*

*Mrs. Bohme feels that Timothy, Melissa, and Matthew are children of above-average intelligence and emotional health who entered an overly academic environment too soon. Their self-esteem, which is largely based on the perception "I am what I can do," is being damaged by demands that they cannot meet. They need more time to develop before they can be receptive to the skills and concepts she is supposed to teach them. Normal maturation processes will lead to significant improvement in their impulse control, confidence, and motivation to read. However, Mrs. Bohme knows that if she were allowed to implement a curriculum with a range of learning experiences that could accommodate individual differences, kindergarten could be a positive rather than a stressful learning experience for children like Timothy, Melissa, and Matthew. Their natural growth process could be respected and enhanced, rather than distorted by external factors.*

Mrs. Bohme's classroom is typical of many kindergartens throughout the nation. The curriculum is not suited to the abilities and varied levels of the children and has, in the words of kindergarten teacher Carol Hoffman, "gone astray." As a result, large numbers of students face the possibility of school failure.

According to a study completed by the Educational Research Service, the majority of kindergarten programs today attempt to teach children in formal ways. In many kindergartens, for example, 5 year-olds spend much of their time copying alphabet letters on purple ditto sheets. First graders are often taught addition and subtraction skills using worksheets instead of manipulative objects. In some schools, second graders are required to write persuasive paragraphs and are introduced to mathematical "number lines." Yet in an article entitled "The Resistance to Developmentally Appropriate Educational Practice With Young Children: The Real Issue," David Elkind points out that "few 2nd graders can grasp the notion of infinity implicit in the number line."

The overuse of worksheets has come to symbolize an inappropriate curriculum for young children. The Commission on Education and Public Policy of the National Academy of Education has concluded that "workbook and skill sheet activities consume a large proportion of the time allocated to reading instruction in most American classrooms, despite the fact that there is little evidence that these activities are related to reading achievement."

Early childhood curriculum experts such as Lillian Katz, co-author of ***Engaging Children's Minds,*** also believe that worksheets and workbooks are a waste of children's time. Katz states that the academic nature of worksheets fails to engage student minds sufficiently. An early childhood curriculum should increase children's understanding of the world around them and improve their attitudes about learning. Instead, worksheets often fail to provide learning experiences that are meaningful to children.

## The Negative Effects of Inappropriately Academic Curriculums

When schools expect children to learn skills and concepts before they are intellectually and physically ready, a variety of serious problems result. For example, studies show that developmentally inappropriate curriculums cause students to demonstrate more stress-related behaviors. Such curriculums diminish creativity and enlarge the numbers of remedial and learning disabled students. Moreover, researchers have noted an increase in aggressive behavior, negative attitudes toward learning, and the potential for damage to self-esteem.

Diane Burts and her colleagues at Louisiana State University have completed two studies which document that programs which emphasize workbooks, worksheets, and lock-step instruction produce significantly more stress behaviors in kindergarten children, compared to developmentally appropriate curriculums. Burts also found that boys are particularly vulnerable to inappropriate school practices, displaying more stress-related behaviors in inappropriate classrooms than in appropriate settings. She concluded that since today's children are exposed to a multitude of stressors outside of the school setting, additional stress produced in the classroom may have serious consequences.

In a separate study entitled "Academic Environments in Early Childhood," Professors Kathryn Hirsh-Pasek of Temple University and Marion Tyson of the University of Delaware found that when preschool children were subjected to both parent and school emphasis on academics, they tended to be less creative when they entered school. Also, these children registered more anxiety about tests and soon lost the academic advantage with which they started elementary school. Hirsh-Pasek states that parents and teachers often "forget that play is the work of childhood."

Cross-cultural studies also demonstrate the negative effects of early formal instruction and the benefits of appropriate practice. Reading specialist Paul Ruthman's article, "France," states that France has a state-mandated kindergarten reading program, and some 30 percent of the children have reading problems. However, in Denmark, a country with a high (almost 100 percent) literacy rate, formal instruction is not introduced until the second grade. In fact, the formal teaching of reading and writing in kindergarten is prohibited by law. Mogens Jansen, a Danish reading educator and author of "Denmark," reports that prior the second grade, children experience meaningful language activities and manipulative materials. They are read to, engage in discussions, dictate their own stories, and develop a "sight word" vocabulary (the ability to read a word without sounding out each letter). The Soviet Union, England, and Israel have adopted a similar approach and timetable.

Lawrence Schweinhart and David Weikart of the High Scope Educational Research Foundation conducted a major longitudinal study, which concluded that children taught in "academic" preschools are likely to develop social problems during their teenage years. The children receiving formal, teacher-directed instruction at ages 3 and 4 engaged in twice as many delinquent acts by age 15, compared with those in a traditional, play-oriented nursery school group. Teens with the academic preschool background also demonstrated poor relations with their families, less participation in sports, and less reaching out to others for help when they had personal problems. The non-academic program, because of its emphasis on positive social behavior and meaningful child activity, produced favorable long-term results.

A study by Ron Haskins reached similar conclusions. He followed children taught in an academic preschool for the first two or three years of public school. Elementary teachers rated these children as more aggressive than comparable children who attended traditional daycare centers.

Exposure to excessive amounts of worksheets and other academic activities can also lead to "elementary school burnout" -- an unwillingness to use the skills acquired. In her article, "Motivational Processes Affecting Learning," psychologist Carol Dweck suggests that too much emphasis on skilled performance within an academic curriculum, "may well create the very conditions that have been found to undermine intrinsic interest." Similarly, in "Early Education: What Should Young Children Be Doing?" Lillian Katz explains how early academic pressure may undermine the development of dispositions to use the skills learned.

An inappropriate curriculum consisting of a single teaching method may also increase children's feelings of incompetence. Kindergarten age children, for example, often do not understand the abstract nature of worksheets and blame themselves if they are confused about the task. "I'm stupid," says the child. "I don't know how to do this." The risk of damage to self-esteem is compounded when children are then prematurely and officially labeled as having "learning problems." The real "problem" is an inappropriate curriculum that ignores what is known about the way young children develop.

## Varying Rates of Development among Young Children

There is a wider variation in the rate of development among children ages 4 to 8 than in any other period of childhood. This includes the intellectual, emotional, social, and physical areas, and the extent of the variations can be very deceptive. Whereas 11, 12, and 13 year-olds tend to look very different from each other (some even look like young adults), 4 to 8 year-olds look very much like each other. Yet there is a much greater range of abilities among young children. For example, children in a typical 5 year-old group may have a vocabulary ranging anywhere from 800 to 4,000 words. One child holds a pencil and sees an instrument of communication; another sees it as a rocket ship. One child gets excited when the teacher points out the difference between "b" and "d"; another has no interest in letters.

In reality, a group of young children cannot all succeed when pressed to learn "on schedule." It is unrealistic and unfair to assume all the students in a class will master the same concept or skill at the same time. They need to be allowed to acquire skills at their own individual pace.

As discussed in Chapter 1, Jean Piaget found that as children mature, they pass through four stages of cognitive development: sensorimotor, pre-operational, concrete, and formal operations. Most children cannot truly comprehend certain academic tasks, such as addition and subtraction, until they have reached the concrete operations stage. In many children, this occurs around age 6, but others do not arrive at the same stage until ages 7 or 8. Similarly, some kindergarten and first grade children cannot discriminate between certain phonetic sounds until 7 or 8. They develop reading problems because they are asked to perform tasks that require this skill.

If late-maturing children enter first grade or an academic kindergarten before they have reached the concrete-operations stage, they are likely to have difficulty performing cognitive tasks. Late-blooming 5 or 6 year-olds usually love to be read to but are not interested in being taught to read. All they want to do is play, play, play.

Along with an appropriate curriculum, late maturing children need time for physical growth in order to grow intellectually. In "Growth and Development of the Brain," James Tanner, a Professor of Child Health and Growth at the University of London, writes that there is every reason to believe that the higher intellectual abilities appear "only when maturation of certain structures or (brain) cell assemblies, widespread throughout the (brain) cortex, is complete." He goes on to state that stages of mental functioning are "probably dependent on (i.e., limited by) progressive maturation and organization of the (brain) cortex."

Kurt Fischer, Professor at the University of Denver and co-author of ***Human Development***, has identified several studies suggesting that the general growth of the brain alternates between periods of rapid growth (spurts) and slower increases. Separate studies by Professors Jerome Kagan and Herman Epstein indicate that these spurts occur at the same time children enter one of Piaget's cognitive stages. Whereas age 5 is a time of brain integration rather than rapid brain growth, at about age 6, most children's brains undergo a spurt in growth and function. This corresponds to children's entrance into the concrete operations stage. Anne Soderman, Assistant Professor at Michigan State University, has pointed out in her article, "Formal Education for Four-Year-Olds," that brain spurts increase "the child's ability to attain new levels of learning and accept cognitive challenge." This information corresponds to the work of Edward Zigler that I cited in Chapter l, which shows that fine-motor development, a prerequisite for academic skills, is more dependent on brain maturation than the gross-motor development which precedes it.

## *The Importance of Developmental Maturity*

Studies reviewed by researchers Norman Sprinthall

and Lois Theis-Sprinthall in their article, "The Need for a Theoretical Framework in Educating Teachers," conclude that developmental maturity -- the ability to act responsibly and with compassion --is essential for lifelong success. They found that estimates of developmental maturity, more than high grades and test scores, are the most effective predictors of adult success. Further, psychologist Douglas Heath, a Professor at Haverford College, completed a longitudinal study and concluded that people who function at a high level of success possess additional characteristics of developmental maturity such as emotional health, a sense of humor, energy, enthusiasm, self-discipline and the willingness to take risks.

Several studies support the relationship between school success and maturity. Pediatrician Frances Ilg, co-author of ***School Readiness,*** describes a study from a Connecticut school district which reported that the children assessed as developmentally ready for kindergarten were academically in the top third of their class. The children assessed as developmentally young, however, were in the bottom third.

The Conval, New Hampshire schools also found more problems with children assessed as unready for kindergarten. The children were more likely than those assessed as ready to repeat a grade, to require remedial reading, to have poor peer relations and to demonstrate negative attitudes toward school.

Children who start school before they have the ability to master the curriculum are considered to be "overplaced." Jim Grant, a school readiness consultant and author of ***I Hate School,*** describes the problems of the typically "overplaced" child: "Writing is laborious; he gets tired; he cannot sit through a 20-minute reading lesson or a five-hour day. He often tries to negotiate: 'Hey teacher, can I write just the answers and not the whole sentence?'" Late-blooming children who appear to be "immature" at age 5 find it difficult to sit still, to attend to the teacher's directions, and to work cooperatively in a group.

And, when such children enter most public schools, they are likely to be labeled as slow or disabled learners. In a study entitled, "The Developmental Effect," Robert Wood screened 80 kindergarten children and identified 25 as developmentally young. Immediately after the screening, a school's child-study team diagnosed 19 of the 25 children as learning disabled. Wood's study supports the conclusion of Bruce Bracken, author of "Observing the Assessment Behavior of Preschool Children," who states that it is difficult to differentiate mildly handicapped young children from those who are normal, whereas older children with mild handicaps are more easily identified. Tom Armstrong, author of ***In Their Own Way***, has stated that the U.S. has the "narrowest critical period during which a child has to learn to read or be considered learning disabled."

A critical question is whether the behaviors of developmentally young children are remedied by the passage of time. Recall from Chapter 3 that the longitudinal research study conducted by Stella Chess and Alexander Thomas found that high activity level, distractibility, and shy or slow-to-warm-up behaviors are the result of inborn temperamental traits. While these traits tend to persist throughout childhood, they become less dominant with age and improve when children are thoughtfully managed by adults. Mature behaviors are allowed to emerge when "immature" children are provided with time to grow in non-stressful situations. However, children who start school too soon often become stressed and turn inwards, focusing primarily on their own concerns. With each additional year of overplacement, the pressure increases, and they are likely to become more self-centered and less sensitive to the needs of others.

University of California Professor Paul Mussen has published evidence detailing the psychological characteristics of children who mature more slowly. They exhibit more attention-getting behaviors and are rated by their peers and by trained observers as more restless, talkative and bossy. Also, they are less popular and have lower social status than their age-mates.

### *Gender Differences in Maturation*

Reseachers have found maturational differences to exist between boys and girls, beginning in the early years and continuing throughout childhood. In the book, ***Males and Females,*** Corinne Hutt states that the bone growth of males is slower. The eruption of the permanent teeth, a sign of physical maturity, occurs sooner in girls. Girls enter puberty sooner and generally reach full maturity at an earlier age.

Boys encounter more school problems than girls throughout the elementary years. Diane McGuinness, author of ***When Children Don't Learn,*** summarizes the evidence: 20 to 25 percent of boys are identified for remediation compared to only 5 to 8 percent of girls; 75 percent of reading disabled children are males. Boys are 3 to 5 times more likely to experience the symptoms associated with dyslexia (difficulty with words). Ninety percent of all "hyperactive" classifications are boys. Anne Soderman, author of the article, "Formal Education for Four Year-Olds," maintains that the failure to apply this information in the early years is evident in the "wreckages" at the secondary school level. In high schools, boys outnumber girls 13 to 1 in remedial classes and by as much as 8 to 1 in classes for the emotionally impaired.

Edward Zigler, author of ***Children: Development and Social Issues***, cites studies showing that young girls tend to have an advantage over young boys in fine-motor skills such as writing, drawing, and skipping. Young males are typically better than girls in gross-motor skills such as throwing, catching, and hitting a baseball. At an early age, boys tend to outdistance girls in running and are superior in speed, strength, and agility. But girls demonstrate a more fluent and coordinated fine motor system. This fine motor system includes not only finger dexterity, but speech production, auditory discrimination, and eye movement. Girls are generally better able to follow a line of print, making rapid eye fixations, releases, and refixations.

The fine-motor system is highly related to the development of language and the ability to read. Consequently, a mature fine-motor system is responsible for much of a child's kindergarten readiness and overall success in school. During the primary grades, girls, as a group, demonstrate better reading and spelling achievement than boys.

Through her own studies and those she has reviewed, McGuinness concludes that females are advanced relative to males in speech development all through childhood. Girls have a greater facility for producing accurate speech sounds and using more words in phrases. Also, females are particularly adept at discriminating between complex auditory signals. They consistently show cross-cultural advantages involving auditory sequencing abilities, speech production, and linguistic tasks. In sum, girls are predisposed to learning about the world through verbal communication and, as a result, are better at "being taught."

There is strong evidence that structural differences in the brain are what cause the female advantage. Girls have more efficient organization of neural connections to support language on the left side of the brain, which is the hemisphere specialized for the control of fluent motor action.

Because of greater exposure to testosterone in the uterus, boys experience slower growth of the brain's left hemisphere but more development of the right hemisphere. As a result, boys outperform girls in tasks requiring geometric, mechanical, or spatial skill. Boys demonstrate more accurate judgment of objects in motion, which helps to explain why a larger number of them are fascinated with video games. This imbalance also explains why boys are at greater risk for developmental disorders related to language and speech.

### *Implications of Maturational Differences*

The early advantage demonstrated by girls in articulation, and their general lack of speech problems, suggests that maturational growth in this area is advanced in females. In comparison to girls, boys are more likely to be unready for kindergarten, especially one that is academically demanding. They do better in preschool, in kindergarten and in the primary grades when learning experiences emphasize "hands-on" exploration of objects. Variation of activities, repetition, and opportunities for individual choice are also important. They do less well with teaching methods requiring them to sit for long periods of time.

It is clear that there is a powerful link in the early years between acquiring literacy skills and the development of self-esteem. Bruno Bettleheim, author of ***On Learning to Read,*** states that the children he treated with psychotherapy for emotional disturbance have for the most part been children who failed in their attempts to learn to read. David Elkind says in ***The Hurried Child,*** "Children confronted with the task of learning to read before they have requisite mental abilities can develop long term learning difficulties: damage to self-esteem and negative attitudes toward learning."

All the studies point to a common conclusion -- that children who are developmentally immature, because of inborn temperamental traits and/or slow maturation timetables, suffer in kindergartens which have prescribed, inflexible curriculums. That raises the question of what can be done to protect developmentally young children. One important solution is to design and implement developmentally appropriate curriculums that respond to the wide differences in children ages 4 through 8. Chapter 5 deals with creating a parent-school partnership to accomplish this. However, given the pressures on school systems for high achievement scores and budgetary restraint, implementing a curriculum that accepts and meets the needs of children performing at different levels may take years, if it happens at all. In addition, I believe there will always be some children who need more time to grow, even with the most responsive primary school curriculum.

Several other options have been adopted by school systems to protect children from inappropriate expectations. These options give children the extra time they need for their normal brain growth. The extra-year options include: "developmental" two-year kindergartens, and "transitional" first grades that provide an extra year between kindergarten and first grade. David and Barbara Bjorkland Professors of Psychology at Florida Atlantic University and authors of the article, "Is Your Child Ready for School?" state that "some children need an extra year or so of 'just developing' before they are ready for the demands of modern American schools. If they can be saved from early failure, they quite possibly can be saved from later failure and the accompanying feelings of low self-esteem and poor self-confidence." The positive effects of unpressured learning environments include motivation to learn, increased attention span, and better learning habits.

## The Need to Determine Readiness for Kindergarten

The Bjorklands stress the importance of assessing the readiness of a child about to enter a kindergarten with an inflexible curriculum. I agree wholeheartedly with them. Until the kindergarten through 3rd grade curriculum becomes more developmentally appropriate, the importance of determining maturity for kindergarten and taking steps on the basis of the information obtained can hardly be overstated. According to Robert Lichtenstein and Harry Ireton, authors of ***Preschool Screening,*** "the best case that can be made for screening at the time of kindergarten entry is to determine a child's readiness for school. The objective in this case is not to make a decision whether to provide services, but whether to delay formal education until the child is more mature."

Another equally important reason for screening children prior to kindergarten entrance is to evaluate children's abilities to learn skills and concepts. Those students who demonstrate potential learning problems can be further assessed with diagnostic tests to determine if they have needs which require special education classes.

I recommend using several sources of information when determining kindergarten readiness and making any placement decisions. This concurs with the policy stated in the "NAEYC Position Statement on Standardized Testing of Young Children Three Through Eight Years of Age," that "...decisions that have a major impact on children such as enrollment, retention, or assignment to remedial or special classes should be based on multiple sources of information and should never be based on a single test score." To do otherwise is a violation of appropriate professional practice.

The multi-step readiness assessment procedure I recommend begins with the collection of observational information from parents and pre-school teachers in the form of non-standardized checklists or standardized report forms. It goes on to include a screening "instrument" or assessment, individually administered to children by experienced examiners with training in child development. The readiness screening process concludes with an analysis of the three types of information to determine each child's developmental status.

### *Collecting Information from Parents*

Parents should play a significant decision-making role in determining school readiness. They must always be given the choice to accept or refuse a school's recommendation to place a child in an extra-year classroom. If children are to benefit from the experience, parents need to be in agreement with school administrators and teachers.

Parents are vital sources of information needed to make a placement recommendation. Clearly, they know the most about children's present behavior and past history. Parents can assist the school in its assessment of children's developmental maturity by completing a form which describes the developmental/medical history of the child. The form should include information about pregnancy and prenatal care, as well as the ages at which major developmental milestones -- such as walking, talking, and toilet training -- were reached. Researcher Gerald Wiener investigated the school achievement of prematurely born and low-birth-weight infants and found that both groups of children account for a significant portion of academic failures.

Developmental/medical history questionnaires can be found in screening devices such as Samuel Meisels' ***Early Screening Inventory*** Parent Questionnaire, and the AGS ***Early Screening Profiles*** Health History Survey. Parent views of their children's development and adjustment can also be collected using brief, valid instruments that contain standardized data. One example is Harry Ireton's ***Preschool Development Inventory*** (PDI), which assesses parent observations of children's overall development and problem behaviors. Certain PDI measures are predictive of difficulties in kindergarten. For example, low scores on the general development scale (bottom 10 percent) are associated with a 90 percent chance of poor or below-average performance in kindergarten. Specific problems are also predictive, such as, "talks only in short phrases," "has trouble expressing ideas," "slow to catch on — does not comprehend well," and "immature: acts much younger than age."

Another example is the "Self-Help/Social Profile," a questionnaire that is completed by the child's parent to assess the child's level of development in the areas of communication, daily living skills, socialization, and motor skills. The form is based on the Vineland Adaptive Behavior Scales and can be found in the ***Early Screening Profiles.***

Appendix A of this book contains the non-standardized "Kindergarten Readiness Checklist for Parents" which I have developed based on my observations in classrooms. It deals with areas of Emotional, Physical, Intellectual, and Social Maturity.

Appendix B contains my "Informal Teacher Observation Checklist for 4 to 5 Year-Olds."

Standardized instruments are also available for teachers to evaluate children's social and emotional areas of development. Two such instruments are the "Behavior Survey" and the "Self-Help Profile" located in the ***Early Screening Profiles.*** These forms assess areas such as attention span, frustration tolerance, socialization, and communication.

The accuracy of the information gathered through parent and teacher assessments can be confirmed by administering a screening instrument which is sensitive to children's maturational characteristics.

## *Selecting Screening Instruments*

The selection of screening instruments should be based upon the purpose of the screening as stated by school personnel. The instrument should clearly match the purpose of the screening. If the purpose is to determine levels of developmental maturity, the device chosen should primarily include tasks that assess maturity -- such as the ability to sit still, follow directions, complete a task, self-direct, delay gratification, and cooperate. If the purpose is to identify potential learning problems in children, the instrument selected should contain items which are relevant to success or failure in school -- such as cognition, language, speech, and fine and gross-motor coordination.

Since screening devices are typically used as part of a data- gathering plan to place children in alternative or special programs, they should have documented validity and reliability. Furthermore, instruments should be standardized to allow the results to be compared to a "normative" group, so that there is a scientific basis for determining the range of normal behavior. This normative population should have similar characteristics to the population of children screened.

Careful attention should be paid to the possibility of discriminating against children who are linguistically or culturally different. Instruments should be administered in the native language of the children. Students should not be penalized because a screening device is insensitive to their cultures.

*Screening Instruments to Identify Learning Problems*

Children who suffer from learning difficulties, or from physical or emotional problems, should be accurately identified and remediated as early as possible. Establishment of early screening programs has helped children receive special education, and in many cases, prevented the occurrence of more serious problems. Screening has assisted schools in meeting the federal requirement in Public Law 94-142 to find, identify, and serve handicapped children.

Valid and reliable instruments can be used to screen children by assessing key areas such as cognition (ability to reason, classify, recall, understand concepts), language (expression of thoughts and comprehension of verbal material), fine-motor skills (holding a pencil and cutting), gross-motor skills (hopping, balancing on one foot), and speech (articulation of sounds). The devices are brief and assess a variety of developmental areas. At best, they are "snapshots" of children at the time they are administered. The fact that young children are naturally shy, fearful, and hesitant — especially around adults they may not know — should be a consideration when making placement decisions based on these instruments.

Samuel Meisels, University of Michigan research scientist and author of ***Developmental Screening In Early Childhood***, recommends four screening devices which meet his criteria as valid and reliable. These criteria include the ability to: briefly sample a wide range of developmental rather than academic accomplishments, identify children who may have a learning or handicapping condition that could affect their potential for school success, and cite data about the instrument's validity, reliability and normative population. The four tests are: Frankenburg's ***Denver Developmental Screening Test*** (although some studies show the Denver test overlooks many youngsters at risk); Lichtenstein's ***Minneapolis Preschool Screening Instrument***; ***The McCarthy Screening Test***; and Meisels' own device, the ***Early Screening Inventory***. Another instrument to consider is the "Cognitive Language Profile," found in the AGS ***Early Screening Profiles***.

When the results of screening indicate that a child may have learning problems, diagnostic testing is then provided. Based on the outcomes of diagnostic testing, referral to special education services may result. Meisels maintains that the purpose of diagnostic testing is to identify a child's specific areas of strength and weakness. The nature of the child's problem is determined and the cause suggested. General recommendations are made about placement and teaching strategies. Examples of diagnostic assessment instruments are the ***Stanford Binet Intelligence Scale,*** and the ***Wechsler Preschool and Primary Scale of Intelligence*** (WPPSI). Appendix D of this book contains references to all the instruments I have mentioned in this chapter.

*Screening Instruments to Identify Children Needing Extra Time*

The ***Gesell Developmental Observation Kindergarten Assessment*** has been the most widely used instrument for identifying developmentally young students. Sue Bredekamp and Lorrie Shepard, authors of the article "How Best to Protect Children from Inappropriate School Expectations, Practices, and Policies," state that "the Gesell test, particularly, has helped early childhood teachers gain a better understanding of child development and improve observational skills."

However, several reviewers have found that the Gesell assessment does not meet the "technical standards of the American Psychological Association for validity, reliability, or normative information." Therefore, it is generally agreed the Gesell should not be used as the sole or primary device for making placement decisions.

Two recent studies have shed more light on the value of the Gesell assessment. Richard Walker's study, "The Gesell Screening Examination: Psychometric Properties," concluded that the instrument has "moderate reliability" and "substantial predictive powers." Walker, a Gesell Institute psychologist, found high correlations between results on the Gesell device given to children ages 4 to 6 and a variety of measures administered to the same children at ages 8 to 9. However, he advises that more than one examiner review the test results, and that data from parent and teacher observations also be included. This is to balance the tendency of Gesell-trained examiners, so alert to the harm that inappropriate curriculum does to immature children, to be overprotective.

An investigation of the Gesell's psychometric characteristics by Robert Lichtenstein, author of "Psychometric Characteristics and Appropriate Use of the Gesell School Readiness Screening Test," concluded that although it does not appear to be technically adequate as a primary determinant of grade placement, "it might be useful as one source of information contributing to a developmental assessment." The study also found that the Gesell instrument does indeed support the judgements of classroom teachers. Teacher ratings of learning habits and social maturity were significantly correlated with the Gesell assessment. And the classroom teacher is, according to Lichtenstein, "the single best source of knowledge about a child's educational status."

Schools may want to consider using the adaptive scale from the Gesell assessment. This quantitative version provides an objective scoring method (rather than the examiner's interpretation alone) and consequently increases the instrument's reliability. Lichtenstein's study revealed higher "inter-rater reliability" using objective scoring, in comparison to the clinical scoring method. High inter-rater reliability means that two examiners, observing and scoring the same set of test responses, will arrive at the same results. The validity has proven to be comparable, regardless of the scoring method.

Clearly, the assessment of the developmental maturity of young children requires the consideration of parent and teacher input, along with the results of an assessment instrument. Should the measurement problems associated with maturationally sensitive devices like the Gesell assessment therefore prevent schools from attempting to identify children who may be at risk for school failure? In his article, "Kindergarten Screening and Developmental Placement," Lichtenstein responds to this question:

"It would be backwards logic for this (measurement problems associated with use of the Gesell screening test) to be the deciding factor in the debate. Developmental and educational assessment is not an exact science. The accuracy of placement decisions will be an issue for any program that offers educational options for selected children. The crux of the issue is whether the program has a net beneficial impact. If the academic and personal-social costs of unnecessarily placing a child in an extra year program are indeed great, these errors cannot be afforded. If the benefits far outweigh the costs and the end result is a more developmentally appropriate educational experience for all children, errors must be tolerated and mechanisms for minimizing the impact of inappropriate placement decisions should be explored."

Identifying children who are likely to benefit from extra time to mature is an important first step in providing them with an appropriate education. The second step is to provide a supportive environment which meets their needs for continuous learning experiences. The transitional classrooms described in the next section have been developed precisely for this purpose.

# Transitional Classrooms

Transitional classrooms are designed for normal children who need more time to acquire the maturity, learning habits, motivation, and attention span needed to succeed in school. For such children, the extra year of time and stimulation promotes success and supports positive self-esteem. These children, according to language consultant Katrina deHirsch, develop slowly despite excellent intelligence, and fare better if their school entrance is deferred, "since one more year would make the difference between success and failure."

Participants are placed either in a readiness class prior to kindergarten, or a transitional first between kindergarten and first grade. After completing the readiness class, students enter kindergarten. The transitional first grade is for students who have finished kindergarten but who have been identified as needing extra time before entering first grade.

The additional year is provided within a child-centered environment. In many schools, transitional classrooms provide a model for primary-grade teachers interested in creating a "developmentally appropriate curriculum." Susan Sweitzer, Director of Education and Training for the Gesell Institute in New Haven, Connecticut, recommends the use of transitional classrooms as a "transition" to developmentally appropriate practice. She states: "Until we get to the point where these practices are extended up to the early grades, there have to be some options."

Clearly, children do not languish or "mark time" in these programs. A well-planned transition class is intellectually stimulating. Moreover, the curriculum does not repeat what the students have experienced the year before. Instead, the concepts are extended and elaborated upon. The additional year allows the children to mature in all areas of development while they are exposed to stimulating learning experiences. As Harvard University Professor Jerome Bruner, author of ***Towards a Theory of Instruction,*** says about readiness, the teacher "provides opportunities for its nurture."

As early as 1958, Gordon Liddle and Dale Long reported in the ***Elementary School Journal*** that transitional classrooms were valuable in improving academic performance. During the 1970s and 1980s, students in New Hampshire's public schools consistently achieved the highest scores on the Scholastic Aptitude Test (SAT), even though New Hampshire ranks 50th in state aid to public schools. In ***All Grown Up & No Place To Go,*** David Elkind writes that "In New Hampshire children are not hurried. It is one of the few states in the nation that provides 'readiness' classes for children who have completed kindergarten but who are not yet ready for first grade."

## *Research on Transitional Classrooms*

The extent to which extra-year programs yield academic gains is subject to contrversy, but their beneficial effect on social growth and self-esteem seems clear. As Robert Lichtenstein states in a paper entitled, "Reanalysis of Research on Early Retention and Extra Year Programs," transitional classrooms "offer significant advantages in non-academic areas (e.g., self-concept, adjustment, attitude toward school)."

Jonathan Sandoval, Professor of Education at the University of California, published research in which he studied high school students who years ago had completed the transitional (junior) first grade. The results showed beneficial outcomes. The children placed in the transitional class were superior to the control group on three out of four indicators of academic progress. The students also had favorable attitudes about the transitional program, indicating that the experiences helped them do better socially and emotionally, as well as academically. Sandoval speculated that without the transitional program, they might not have done as well.

Separate studies published by Harry Finlayson, Janet S. Rose, and Joan Chase each indicate that children benefit from extra time or transitional classes as long as their placement is based on maturity rather than low achievement. They also found that the extra time needed to mature should be given early in children's school careers. Finlayson and others conducted studies on student's self-concepts and attitudes towards school. Finlayson reported that the self-concepts of non-promoted children continued to increase during the school year. This conclusion was confirmed by both the children's parents and teachers. Similarly, Ann Reed concluded that transitional first grade students developed more positive attitudes toward school, self, and others, compared to students who qualified for transitional class but went on to first grade. Also, Jordel Rihl found that starting school in a transitional class had a positive effect on the development of sixth graders' self-concepts.

Several doctoral dissertations have concluded that transitional classrooms have an overall beneficial effect on developmentally young children. John Caggiano's study concluded that students judged "not ready" for first grade are more likely to adjust positively and more likely to experience school success if provided sufficient time to mature in transitional classrooms. Gretchen

Kilby also found that placements in learning disability programs were significantly less for transitional class children than for children of equal maturity who did not attend.

The most informative evaluation of transitional classrooms was conducted by the Brevard County, Florida, schools. Brevard began its school readiness programs in the early 1980s, and its research found much parental satisfaction with the program. Parents responding to a district-wide survey indicated overwhelming support of the program.

Follow-up studies have found that Brevard students participating in the transitional kindergarten and first grade classes were achieving equal to the district's average test scores by the end of the third grade. As a group, these students were functioning 25 to 30 percentile points above the national average in reading and math by the end of third grade.

In a study completed by the public schools of neighboring Broward County, Florida, children assessed as developmentally young who entered a transitional first grade class (Group One), were compared with children also assessed as developmentally young, but who went to a regular first grade class (Group Two). The study, titled "Prefirst Grade: A Longitudinal Study," concluded that by the fourth grade, Group One children scored significantly higher on achievement tests and social measures of peer acceptance than did Group Two.

The St. Charles Parish (County) Public Schools in Louisiana have followed the progress of their developmentally placed students through the sixth grade and have observed a dramatic increase in achievement scores at each grade level. Since instituting the developmental kindergarten program in 1981, there have been fewer discipline problems, fewer children in special education programs, and fewer retentions in later grades. Also, school nurses report fewer visits to their offices.

The Oxford Primary Schools in New York State instituted readiness and transitional classes in 1979, when 22 percent of their third graders needed remedial help with math. By 1988, only 2 percent of the third graders required remedial math assistance. The percentage of remedial reading students also dropped from 24 to 6 percent during the same period of time. Similar success stories have occurred in the Springfield Local Schools in Lucas County, Ohio, and in the public schools of Lawrenceville and Haddonfield, both of which are in New Jersey.

A much publicized 1985 study, conducted by Professors Lorrie Shepard and Mary Lee Smith, concluded that transitional classrooms, though not harmful, do not boost academic performance in schools as had been expected. They conducted a study of 80 children in Boulder, Colorado, which led them to state there were no clear advantages to having an extra year of school prior to first grade. However, even they found a slight difference in achievement test scores in favor of the extra-year students. And, Shepard and Smith's published conclusions omitted the positive social-emotional effects of giving children more time to grow. Their original study includes figures showing that in every area of "Teacher Ratings" (reading, math, social maturity, learner self-concept, and attention), the group receiving the extra year (the "retained" group) scored higher. Most important, the figures were especially higher in the areas of social maturity and learner self-concept. The Shepard and Smith study also does not separate those children who repeated kindergarten from those who were placed in transition programs. All were part of the "retained" group.

Shepard and Smith contend in their book, ***Flunking Grades***, that the study of extra-year programs is "limited by the lack of systematic investigation of long-term effects." However, they do not mention Betty McCarty's eight-year study of the effect of kindergarten non-promotion on developmentally immature children. McCarty's results indicated that non-promotion of developmentally young kindergarten children had a positive effect on subsequent levels of peer acceptance, academic attitude, classroom adjustment, and academic achievement.

In general, studies which have reported negative effects of transitional classrooms, such as those described in Gilbert Gredler's article, "Transitional Classes," studied children who were academically at risk. It must, however, be remembered that a transitional program is not intended for remediation. It is developmental, and therefore is based on the premise that children have not yet acquired academic skills.

More than 25 studies of transitional classroom programs are summarized in Dr. James K. Uphoff's ***School Readiness and Transition Programs: Real Facts From Real Schools***. According to Uphoff, these studies show that students in transitional classes have at least done as well as fellow students in regard to academic achievement in later years, and in many cases they have surpassed the national averages. The classes have also produced very positive benefits in regard to student self-concept, and emotional and social maturity. Further, there has been overwhelmingly strong satisfaction and support for transitional classes among parents whose children participated in such classes.

## *The Transitional Class Debate*

Transitional classrooms have become a controversial issue. Supporters view them favorably because they help children who might do poorly in a rigid, academic curriculum, by providing instead the opportunity to be successful in a more relaxed, developmentally appropriate environment. Extra-year programs are therefore seen as a clear alternative to grade retention.

Critics, however, argue that such classrooms often become a "dumping ground" for children with low abilities and emotional problems. There may be merit to this argument if schools use transitional classrooms for children who have handicaps or learning problems, or if they inaccurately identify children using techniques and instruments which are insensitive to maturational factors.

Critics also argue that transitional classrooms are a form of retention in which children are stigmatized because they do not progress directly to the next grade. However, as Dr. James Uphoff writes in the article "Proving Your Program Works," "Clearly there is a tremendous difference between a child whose school experience has been one of failure, and a child in a success-oriented program providing time to grow."

The National Association for the Education of Young Children (NAEYC) opposes transitional classrooms because it believes lack of school readiness is most often due to rigid, inappropriate curriculums. NAEYC argues the schools should change so children do not need extra time in order to succeed. They have proposed a shift toward more developmentally appropriate practices in kindergarten and in the primary grades as a way of reducing the large number of children deemed to be unready for school. In an NAEYC publication titled, ***Kindergarten Policies: What Is Best for Children***, co-author Johanne Peck states that instead of increasing the age of school entry, "resources and energy should instead be redirected to offering a good program." Many supporters of this position feel that transitional programs impede progress toward the goal of creating appropriate curriculums for all students.

There may be some truth to this, but I am not aware of any hard data which supports this position. And, eliminating readiness and transition classes does not mean that a school will quickly or even eventually implement a developmental curriculum. Many schools will have great difficulty changing to a system that requires additional teacher training and smaller class sizes.

Robert Wood, director of the Northeast Foundation for Children and co-author of ***A Notebook for Teachers***, believes that kindergarten teachers are hard-pressed to create a curriculum that meets the individual needs of children, when the developmental age range in a typical class may vary as much as three years. In an average kindergarten, where some children behave like 4 year-olds and others like 5 or 6 year-olds, responding to individual student needs requires high levels of diagnostic teaching skills and more specialized preparation than teachers normally receive.

School personnel interested in providing a developmentally appropriate curriculum for all students realize it is a worthwhile goal that may take time to achieve. In the meantime, many of these schools have established, or are considering, transitional classrooms. To be effective, such programs must be carefully implemented. The following series of guidelines can help parents and educators prepare for success.

## *Strategies for Protecting Children from School Failure through Transitional Classes and Other Extra-Year Options*

**Children are accurately identified for placement in transitional classrooms as early as possible.** If a child is developmentally young at age 5, the best time to provide the extra year of growth is before kindergarten.

**Multiple sources of information are used when making placement decisions, including valid, reliable assessment instruments that are sensitive to maturational levels.**

**Teachers, parents, administrators, and community members are made aware that transitional classroom students are normal children who develop more slowly than others.** Late-bloomers require time and assistance to accomplish perceptual motor tasks. They may daydream or have short attention spans, but they are not special education students.

**Parents, teachers, and community members are educated about a school placement program through the use of speakers, printed material, video and audiotapes.** Parents need to understand that the most important purpose of a transitional classroom is to benefit children's self-esteem, social growth, and attitudes toward learning. They should be in agreement with this goal. A parents-as-partners approach works best in this regard, and it should include information on how to explain placement in a readiness kindergarten or transitional first grade class to children.

**Steps are taken to ensure that special-needs children are not overlooked.** Special education services should not be delayed when transitional classes are available. Transitional classes should be prevented from becoming a "dumping ground" for children who need remediation or special education. Such children should be given one-to-one instruction by educators who have been trained in teaching strategies which develop perceptual-motor and language skills. The materials for this type of program can be obtained from the Early Prevention of School Failure organization in Peoria, IL.

**The transitional classroom serves as a model for a developmentally appropriate curriculum for all students.** Children should not repeat the kindergarten curriculum in the transitional first grade. Instead, their learning should be extended. The goal is for other primary grade classrooms to look more like the transitional class. The existence of the transitional class should not be used as an excuse to maintain or increase the abstract, accelerated, and academic nature of the curriculum.

## *Strategies to Protect Children from School Failure in the Absence of Extra-Year Options*

Starting in the late 1980s, a number of state departments of education began discouraging the use of transitional classrooms and retention practices by threatening to eliminate funding for school districts adopting such practices. This type of action does not bode well for the late-maturing child, especially when there is no corresponding allocation to schools for training, support, or resources to change to developmentally appropriate curriculums. On the contrary, most states are still requiring public schools to administer standardized achievement tests in the early grades, which further block movement toward a responsive, age-appropriate curriculum. When schools eliminate both transitional classrooms and retention policies, and do not create a developmentally appropriate curriculum, these vulnerable late-blooming children suffer. They become victims of budgetary pressures and the refusal to acknowledge child development needs.

In such situations, it may help to keep in mind other programs and teaching interventions that can be used to reduce school failure.

**Establish a "young fives" preschool program which provides an extra year to grow in a supportive learning environment.**

**Establish a preschool program within the public school for 4 year-old children who need language development.** Because poor language skills are one of the signals for future learning difficulties, early intervention can help children who do not express themselves or understand others well. A program that provides stimulation for language development, rather than direct teaching, will give these children the additional experiences they need. This can help offset the maturation time they are losing.

**Use teacher judgment to identify and help children who are developmentally young.** Without labeling these children as needing remediation, give them some extra help. Ask if children are displaying low academic skills because they are at risk for a learning disability, or just because they are developing more slowly?

**Increase tutoring and one-on-one instructional programs.** One effective instructional program for first graders is called "Reading Recovery," which is described by Marie Clay in ***The Early Detection of Reading Difficulties.***

**Implement cooperative learning and peer tutoring programs which allow children to learn from one another.** Read David Johnson's ***Cooperation in the Classroom.*** Also see the strategies for fostering social development in the first chapter of this book.

**Support a parent education program and the active parent involvement in the education of their children.** It is critical that parents and schools work in partnership to protect children from school failure from the beginning. The more parents understand and accept their children, the more impact they can have on them. One program which helps parents support their children is called EPIC (Effective Parenting Information for Children), which was developed by the Buffalo, NY public schools.

No one person or group can be held responsible for making curriculums incompatible with our knowledge of how children develop and learn, but everyone is responsible for doing something about it. The twin priorities are to protect developmentally young children from the adverse effects of inappropriate curriculums, and extend the developmentally appropriate model used in transitional programs throughout the entire primary curriculum. This can only be accomplished through teacher support, teacher training and parent education. Chapter 5 explains how parents and teachers can best support the design and implementation of a developmentally appropriate curriculum.

*Practice* 5

# Support a developmentally appropriate curriculum

*In a public elementary school's kindergarten classroom, the teacher is getting ready to read a "big book" as part of a whole language literacy program. She asks the children to look carefully at the title and cover, and then predict what the book is going to be about, while she carefully records their responses on a large piece of paper. The text is read by the teacher, after which the children dramatize the story. As the week progresses, the children create their own big books, filling them with drawings and their own writing, including scribbles and invented spelling. They then share their books with each other and the teacher, before taking them home to show their parents. They also have discussions in class about topics related to the book, use crafts materials to recreate some of the characters and objects depicted in the book, and write about the experiences in their journals.*

*Six year-olds in a private primary school choose from among several learning center activities. One child is creating a collage about airplanes, while another child who has recently traveled over a bridge uses blocks to reconstruct it. On the other side of the classroom, the teacher is working with a small group of children who are closely observing the movements of a garden snake. She writes a question on the board: "How do snakes move?" A list of "predictors" is written on the left side of a chart, leaving the right side for reporting results of the observation. Some children draw the movements of the snake while others write words and sentences.*

These two vignettes are typical examples of teachers using developmentally appropriate practices in the classroom. The students are learning subjects and skills by building upon personal experiences in a variety of ways. Children are encouraged to think creatively, manipulate concrete materials, and make choices about what they will do. According to Sue Bredekamp, editor of ***Developmentally Appropriate Practice In Early***

*Childhood Programs Serving Children From Birth Through Age 8,* developmentally appropriate practices (DAP) are implemented when teachers' methods and materials are based on an understanding of children's development.

Educators who implement DAP respect the wide variability in levels of development among young children of the same chronological age. Consequently, they expect and plan for students who have different learning styles and perform at different levels of ability. They also understand that children learn best in a holistic manner, rather than by focusing on isolated skills. Young children do not say to themselves, "Now I'm doing social studies, next I'll learn math." When learning is based on meaningful experiences, children engage in activities which combine numerous subjects.

Teachers support this natural way of learning by using DAP concepts and methods to organize their curriculum. These concepts and methods, which will be explained in more detail on the following pages, include: **learning modalities, concrete materials**, a **whole language** approach, subject integration through **core experiences, theme projects**, and **learning center** activities.

## Learning Modalities

Children absorb information by hearing, seeing and touching -- which are more formally known as auditory, visual, and tactile/kinesthetic modalities or channels. While most children use all three of these modalities to some extent, individual children usually acquire skills and concepts better through one channel than the others. Balancing the learning environment, by diversifying materials and techniques to include all three channels, is essential to reach all the students in a class and create a developmentally appropriate curriculum.

Some children, for example, excel at listening and recalling what has been discussed. Their strength lies in their auditory modality. They tend to be good readers because they easily discriminate between letter sounds. An appropriate curriculum that recognizes their auditory discrimination skills includes the opportunity to learn to read through a phonics approach (studying the relationship between letters and sounds). In general, older children are more likely to be strongly auditory than younger students.

There is another group of children who possess a strong visual modality and so excel at remembering what they see. An appropriate curriculum contains many visually appealing materials to support this learning style. Visually oriented children learn best through pictures, charts, graphs, maps, and other visual displays. They have better recall of words that are written on a chalkboard or large piece of paper. The preferred method of reading instruction for them is the "look-say" approach, because it shows the patterns of whole words and phrases. Language experience activities -- such as writing stories, reading books, and chanting choral readings -- are also effective.

Because their auditory and visual abilities are still developing, the majority of young children are primarily tactile and kinesthetic learners. They prefer to touch, manipulate, and move their bodies. Studies by Marie Carbo, co-author of ***Teaching Students to Read Through Their Individual Learning Styles***, conclude that beginning readers and poor readers tend to be strongly tactile/kinesthetic and have less of an inclination to learn visually and auditorially. They prefer to learn by touching, since they remember words by tracing and "feeling" them. These students need to work with sandpaper letters as they learn their sounds, read high interest stories, act out plots and characters, draw pictures, and write or dictate stories. Their learning is best motivated by books with colorful illustrations. Relying solely on a phonics approach with tactile/kinesthetic learners is ineffective, because it does not utilize their dominant modality. On the other hand, books with colorful illustrations engage them.

Many teachers present information to children based on their own personal modality strength. As a result, only a portion of the students learn in an optimal way. In a class dominated by teacher talk, worksheets, and a phonics-based reading approach, the students who are primarily auditory will do better than those who are predominantly visual or tactile/kinesthetic. The latter children may have difficulty understanding and keeping up with the work.

However, if tactile/kinesthetic learners are exposed to a variety of teaching materials and methods as they mature physically, they gradually develop secondary modality strengths which complement and enhance their dominant channel. Eventually, their modalities become mixed. This is advantageous because they are then able to learn facts and concepts regardless of how the teachers present information.

## *Creating a Balanced Learning Environment*

A good rule for teachers to remember is: "teach to a different learning modality every day." Below is a chart that describes the characteristics of each modality and a related list of teaching ideas. All children can benefit from exposure to these varied learning experiences.

| Modality | Student Characteristics | The teacher can.. |
|---|---|---|
| Auditory | Shows verbal ability<br>Possesses a good memory<br>Enjoys being read to | Allow time to read<br>Use tape recorded books<br>Tell stories<br>Use word games<br>Encourage memorization of poems and short stories<br>Brainstorm (ask questions/list ideas)<br>Encourage poetry and creative story writing<br>Use phonics approach to teach reading |
| Visual | Motivated by visual displays<br>Impatient with activities involving a long story with no pictures | Use bulletin boards and art projects<br>Use charts, pictures, and maps<br>Use guided imagery (pictures in the mind to motivate writing)<br>Use wall/table displays of projects and objects<br>Use films and videotapes<br>Perform demonstrations<br>Sequence pictures to tell a story<br>Use a sight approach/language experience to teach reading<br>Use mazes, geoboards, magnifying glasses<br>Encourage designing and inventing |

| | | |
|---|---|---|
| Tactile/ Kinesthetic | Enjoys moving/ touching objects<br>May show little interest in reading print | Read/act out action stories<br>Make and build dioramas<br>Use blocks, chips, rods to teach math<br>Use movement, creative drama to teach concepts<br>Encourage writing letters and words with sand, clay, and paint<br>Use woodworking/sewing<br>Allow children to act out words as they are formed |

## Concrete Materials

A developmentally appropriate early childhood curriculum contains an abundance of concrete (manipulative) materials such as blocks, cubes, rods, puzzles, cards, arts and crafts, and science equipment. When children under the age of 8 are thoughtfully guided by teachers to interact with these materials, their ability to develop logical thought is supported. Learning with concrete objects is essential if children are to be successful in understanding more complex concepts as they progress through school.

The arrangement and rearrangement of objects in the real world helps children understand abstract concepts in their later years. Manipulating and seeing relationships between objects in early childhood allows students to manipulate words and numbers more easily in their middle childhood and teenage years. This rearrangement of symbols in the mind is the essence of real thought. In the book ***Mindstorms***, MIT Mathematics Professor Seymour Papert describes the positive relationship between his own early experiences with gears and other manipulative objects, and their influence on his ability to understand abstract concepts as an adult.

Children who have limited experience with concrete materials in the early years tend to have difficulty grasping abstract concepts in the upper grades. Worksheets are too abstract for young children and concerned only with correct answers. Mental activity is more likely to be stimulated when the teacher introduces objects that can be observed, compared, and classified.

For example, a first or second grade teacher can introduce the topic of land transportation to children by arranging a display of plastic cars, buses, trucks, wagons, trains, and motorcycles. Because the children are able to observe and manipulate the different types of transportation, they are better able to notice and describe what they see. They then can compare and analyze the similarities and the differences. This requires them to group or categorize the models, thereby stimulating the growth of concept development.

After the children physically classify the models into different categories, they can use "divergent thinking" to play at being inventors, by literally "reinventing the wheel." They can create and name, through drawings or constructions, their own unique forms of land transportation. Or, they may be invited to think divergently by seeing relationships between certain forms of transportation and unrelated objects. How, for example, is a car like a cloud?

When children evaluate, they are practicing what is considered the highest level of thinking. The teacher can encourage them to make judgments about the best types of land transportation, based on simple criteria. The students can also play the game called "Prove It," which requires them to provide evidence that a certain means of transportation is better than others. Thus, they are preparing themselves for a lifetime of decision-making.

## A Whole Language Approach

Learning to read and write is difficult for children when letters, words, and sentences are presented without a meaningful context -- that is, without being related to their life experiences and interests. Meaningful contexts motivate learning. A whole language philosophy emphasizes high-interest children's literature, precisely because its meaning engages children's thought processes. As a result, they learn to read and write concurrently.

A whole language classroom provides easy access to literature in the form of big books, picture books, fairy tales, fables, and brief biographies. Every classroom is, in a sense, a mini-library. The students are enveloped in a carefully designed, print-rich environment containing labels, signs, and captions that stimulate them to read, write, and verbally interact. Dr. Dorothy Strickland, co-editor of ***Emerging Literacy: Young Children Learn to Read and Write,*** further recommends daily read-aloud periods in which teachers or children read quality fiction and non-fiction to the rest of the class.

Teachers using a whole language approach avoid relying on traditional basal readers as the essential materials in the reading program. Former Secretary of Education William Bennett, writing in ***First Lessons: A***

*Report on Elementary Education in America,* is critical of most basal textbooks. He calls them poorly written and of dubious literary quality. The overuse of "readability formulas" and small words which are systematically repeated rob the stories of literary beauty.

A number of controlled studies have directly compared whole language reading instruction with basal reader and worksheet instruction. The landmark study by Dorothy Cohen in 1968 found that second grade students who were given a literature-based program showed significant increases in word knowledge, reading comprehension, and quality of vocabulary, compared to a control group which was given basal readers and work sheets. The literature-based program mainly consisted of children being read aloud to, followed by meaning-related activities and teacher encouragement of individual re-reading at any time. Subsequent studies by Bernice Cullinan in 1974 and Nancy Larrick in 1987 re-enforced Cohen's findings.

A whole language philosophy also rejects the practice of placing children into reading groups based on ability. In kindergarten and first grade, ability grouping is likely to create several problems. First, it is difficult to accurately assess reading levels given children's different rates of development and lack of test-taking abilities. Children who are developmentally or chronologically younger may be inaccurately identified as poor readers and placed in the "low" group. These children may actually be "late bloomers" whose abilities change dramatically in a short period of time. Once labeled, however, the "low" group status may become internalized and develop into a self-fulfilling prophecy that unnecessarily cripples children for their entire life.

According to the Wisconsin Center for Educational Research, there is a strong tendency for the "low" group children to slow each other down. When brought together, they do not interact productively. The ***Education Letter***, published by the Harvard Graduate School of Education, reviewed research in this area and found that students in the low groups tend to interrupt the teacher continually and sabotage one another's academic efforts. Children in the "high" groups have been documented as cooperating on assigned work, encouraging groupmates to study, and tending to accelerate each other. However, many of them develop anxiety about demotion into a lower group.

In whole language classrooms, teachers use a variety of grouping strategies, which change frequently and are not based solely on ability. There are whole-group lessons such as story readings, group singing, and class discussions. Small groups are also organized at times for specific skill instruction, cooperative learning, and learning center projects. Teachers also meet individually with students to tutor, listen to the retelling of a story, take dictation, or assess progress.

## Subject Integration Through Core Experiences

A whole language philosophy allows teachers to easily integrate a variety of subject matter areas with reading and writing. Dr. Strickland recommends that teachers plan to make a set of four "core experiences" available every day:

1) **inquiry activities**
2) **shared reading and writing**
3) **individual drawing and writing**

4) **independent reading, reading aloud, and sharing**

**Inquiry activities** allow the children to manipulate materials and ideas, based on a science, social studies, or math problem that is posed. If the week's theme is "sound," for example, a drum, guitar, alarm clock, tuning fork, and glass of water are left on a table. The problem might be, "How can we create sounds with these objects?" At various times during the week, the children actively participate in learning the concept that sounds are made through vibrations. They create sounds, listen, observe, conduct experiments, and classify objects and pictures. The children engage in high level thinking by responding to questions such as "Which sounds are similar? What would the world be like if there were no sounds? Which sounds are beautiful?"

**Shared reading and writing** is a planned "core experience" which follows the inquiry activity and allows the children to progress from concrete to abstract experiences. The teacher (and the children when possible) read from a book related to the inquiry activities together. They then create a chart describing their observations about the topic. Each child's comments are written on the chart, followed by his or her name. Group readings of poems or big books can also be part of this process. After reading the poem or story together, the children are guided through a "text analysis." They look for letters and words they recognize, repetitions, punctuation marks, and beginning and ending sounds.

Young children enjoy big books such as ***Mrs. Wishy Washy*** and ***I Was Walking Down the Road***, because these books provide predictability, rhyming, and repetition. During and following the story, children answer such questions as: Who were the main characters? Where did the story take place? How did the story begin? Are there other characters? What is the problem? How is it solved? How did it end? What was the fun part? The teacher creates charts by writing down the children's responses to the questions next to their names.

**Individual drawing and writing** comprise a third core experience. Opportunities for expression are first provided through drawing or painting pictures. This is followed by the children describing what they have created to a teacher, who writes the description on a separate piece of paper. Both the drawings and dictated stories are displayed for all to view and read. Individual drawing and writing can also be a "literature extension" experience in which favorite scenes or characters from a story are drawn or described.

As I explained in the section of Chapter 1 on physical development, children as young as 4 can write their own stories by scribbling and using invented spelling. Charles Temple, co-author of ***The Beginnings of Writing***, provides an example of how some 4 year-olds string letters together to write whole sentences, such as "M B E W W M L nt." The child reads it back as "My baby was with me last night." Temple recommends the use of invented spelling to encourage the enjoyment of writing until ages 7 and 8, when most children are ready to focus on correct spelling.

**Independent reading, reading aloud, and sharing** are a fourth "core experience" recommended by Dr. Strickland. Every classroom needs a well-stocked library in addition to the school library. Time is set aside for children to browse and read through story and information books, including smaller versions of big books. Teachers also read story books aloud and the children then act them out. A story that children enjoyed as part of a shared reading experience can later be read independently or to each other.

## Theme Projects

Teachers can integrate reading, language arts, social studies, math, science, music, and art by organizing the curriculum around themes that children participate in selecting. Animals, plants, Native Americans, weather, the ocean, and nutrition are examples of high-interest themes. Each theme can last a week or more, depending on the degree of student interest. The teacher can read a story related to the theme each day, in addition to designing learning experiences which cover various subject areas that are related to the theme.

For example, a kindergarten teacher planning activities around a month-long theme on animals decides to study teddy bears. She asks the students to bring their own teddy bears to school for the day. She then reads the children a story called ***The Biggest Bear*** by Lynn Ward. A discussion of the story follows. The children are asked questions that stimulate thinking, such as "What would happen if your teddy bears began to grow and got very large?" and "How are your teddy bears all the same and how are they different?"

For the next two weeks, the students spend some time each day engaged in teddy bear activities. They create a mural of a teddy bear family. They recreate their own teddy bears using clay and Tinker Toys. They give their teddy bears names, draw pictures, and dictate stories. They classify the bears based on size and color; then count and order them from smallest to biggest. Each bear is measured and graphs are created.

The students sing teddy bear songs, make up rhymes, listen to poetry, and write in their own teddy bear books, which they read to each other.

Another example of subject integration involves a theme on foods, which begins with the teacher reading aloud ***Chocolate Fever*** by Robert K. Smith. After a discussion about the importance of establishing moderate eating habits, the teacher shows the children a picture of a sandwich. She asks the class to describe what they see and write down their comments on chart paper. The children then identify the ingredients they would want on a sandwich, and these are also recorded.

The teacher sends a letter home to parents explaining the learning experience and inviting them to bring specific ingredients to a "Sandwich Party" that week. At the party, the students measure each child's sandwiches and graph the results. They sample the variety of sandwiches and vote on their favorite. The results are recorded, with the students describing the taste and smell of each sandwich. Following the best part -- eating the sandwiches -- the students create stories and draw pictures of "The Day My Sandwich Took Over the World."

Many other creative ideas that integrate subject matter areas can be found in ***Transitions: From Literature To Literacy***, by Regie Routman.

The project approach, as described by Dr. Lillian Katz in her book, ***Engaging Children's Minds***, consists of exploring a theme through in-depth study. A typical project is planned in advance and explores something real that children can relate to their lives, such as "the hospital," "building a house," "construction sites," or "the bus that brings us to school." A project might last anywhere from a week to several weeks, and it involves active teaching strategies such as a visit to a construction site, building models, creating paintings, asking questions, and discussing pictures. The students may engage in dramatic play, make books, and create graphs, with all their work being displayed.

According to Dr. Katz, a large body of research supports the project approach as an appropriate way to enhance children's intellectual and social development. Projects incorporate activities that develop skills and concepts in a meaningful context. Moreover, they encourage children to learn by using all three of their modalities -- visual, auditory, and tactile/kinesthetic.

## Learning Center Activities

Learning centers are carefully designed sections of a classroom which contain a variety of materials related to a particular group of subjects or learning experiences. Learning center activities emerge from children's involvement with projects that utilize the resources available in the centers.

In the writing center, for example, students can prepare the text for books they are creating. In the art center, they can make covers and illustrations for their books. The science center contains materials for conducting experiments, as well as animals or plants to observe, and books about science. A dramatic play area provides props and costumes which help children to engage in role-playing. Other centers may be organized around reading, listening, math, science, social studies, puzzles, and puppets.

Each center also contains teacher-made descriptions of projects for students. In the math center, one project might involve children working in pairs and cooperatively building a two-story structure. The next project is to count the blocks used and estimate how many are needed for a third story.

According to Barbara Day, author of ***Early Childhood Education,*** learning centers promote the development of academic, communication and social skills, as well as positive self-esteem, independence, and values such as respecting and helping others. Day summarized the research on learning centers and found them to be effective when they are based on clearly defined goals, well-managed, and include a variety of appropriate materials.

Books such as ***Creating A Learning-Centered Classroom*** by Harold Blake, and ***Caring Spaces, Learning Places*** by Jim Greenman, are useful resources for organizing learning centers.

## Implementing Curriculum Change

Teachers and parents can work together to change a school curriculum so that it is developmentally appropriate. Numerous school districts around the nation have successfully done so and are willing to share their process and materials. Resource materials abound on both the national and local levels. This section highlights many of them, and Appendix D contains a carefully researched list.

Any concerned citizen can be the catalyst for change. Grassroots movements are strongest when they begin with people who are most directly affected -- in this case, parents and teachers. Interested citizens can form a study group in order to familiarize themselves more deeply with the subject of developmentally appropriate practices. They can then go as a group to school boards and parent associations to propose the formation of an official Early Childhood Education Committee composed of representative teachers, parents, school board members, administrators, and early childhood education experts. In those communities where curriculum change has occurred, teachers and parents have been involved in the change process, including decision-making and evaluation, from the beginning. Their alliance is best characterized as a school-parent partnership.

It must be remembered that the change process takes time and may involve overcoming several hurdles. One hurdle is the resistance of some teachers and parents to developmentally appropriate practices. Many teachers of young children already feel overworked. Each year, they are told to add a new subject into the curriculum: computers, drug education, ecological and global education, and so on. They may perceive the change to DAP as one more requirement that is being forced upon them and for which they have little time. Moreover, many teachers have been trained in traditional approaches and may resist DAP because they are unfamiliar with its goals and methods. Administrators and school board officials may feel the same way, and they may be under pressure from state departments of education to improve students' scores on standardized achievement tests.

Parents may be uncomfortable with teaching practices different from their own schooling. Some may believe that early formal instruction and competition is good or necessary for children. It may be helpful to remember that resistance is a natural part of the change process, and that the greater the change, the greater the resistance.

## Strategies for Supporting A Developmentally Appropriate Curriculum

An Early Childhood Education Committee takes action in at least five major ways. Its members:

1) **become informed about DAP**
2) **develop on-going parent education and involvement projects**
3) **support teacher education and recognition**
4) **conduct on-going curriculum evaluation and review**
5) **examine their school's written philosophy**

I have compiled the following suggestions from my research on successful school change, and organized them around the five major courses of action listed above.

### *Become Informed About DAP*

**Read national reports such as *Right From The Start*.** This publication, from the National Association of State Boards of Education (NASBE), calls for the creation of early childhood units within the schools. Each unit focuses on children age 4 to 8 and is organized to stimulate collaboration among teachers, administrators, and parents, as well as to promote learning and development in young children. The report affirms the importance of specialized knowledge of child development and recommends that the training of teachers, administrators and parents be oriented to the unique needs of young children. NASBE agrees with the developmentally appropriate curriculum approach defined by the National Association for the Education of Young Children (NAEYC). They support an "intellectually stimulating environment" in which the teacher has a good understanding of child development, and is skilled in both observing children and interacting with them in ways that extend their thinking.

**Urge school board members to separately administer the educational program for children ages 4 through 8.** The supervisor for this early childhood unit should be highly knowledgeable about child development, early childhood curriculum, and effective teaching methods.

**Obtain publications about school systems which have changed to developmentally appropriate practices.** In Maine, the department of education disseminates a manual entitled *Big Book for Educators: Developmentally Appropriate Practice — A Guide to Change.* Written by Maizie Argondizza, early elementary consultant for the Maine Department of Educational and Cultural Services, the manual is a "tool for reflection" aimed at assisting traditionally trained teachers in examining their own methods and philosophies in relation to DAP. The manual provides information on using instructional strategies that promote cooperation instead of competition, and it emphasizes the use of intrinsic motivation when teaching young children. Several Maine school systems, such as those in Scarborough and Freeport, offer developmentally appropriate curriculums as part of a "choice model" for parents. The Portland, Oregon schools have produced a similar guide titled, "A Self-Study Document for Pre-Kindergarten Through Second Grade," by Rebecca Severeide.

Several public schools across the nation have been spotlighted in the national media for their success with primary grade curriculum changes that support child development principles. The Greenbrook School in South Brunswick, New Jersey was featured in the April 17, 1989 issue of ***Newsweek,*** in an article entitled "How Kids Learn" by Barbara Kantrowitz and Pat Wingert. The South Brunswick teachers generally supported the curriculum changes because they were part of the process from the beginning. Their classrooms feature concrete materials, a whole language approach to reading instruction, and a curriculum that "fits the child" instead of making the child fit the school.

The Primary Integrated Curriculum of the Jefferson County, Colorado Public Schools was described in the April, 1984 issue of ***Educational Leadership.*** The article by Marge Melle, "Balanced Instruction Through an Integrated Curriculum," describes the first and second grade integration of science, social studies, health, environmental and career education. A similar model was adopted by the Fairfax County, Virginia schools and reported in an article by Thomas McGarry, entitled "Integrating Learning for Young Children." Primary grade teachers attended four full-day in-service training sessions scheduled throughout the year. They developed integrated units of instruction and received on-going support from supervisors.

Also Dr. James K. Uphoff's books, ***Dialogues on Developmental Curriculum*** and ***Changing to a Developmentally Appropriate Curriculum — Successfully,*** provide in-depth case studies of schools which have implemented DAP.

**Call NAEYC information services (1-800-424-2460) for other information about schools which have successfully created DAP classrooms.** Visits to the schools mentioned above, or others like them, may also be possible.

**Become familiar with publications that report on the latest developments in educational issues of national interest.** *Education Week, Phi Delta Kappan,* and *Educational Leadership* regularly carry articles on DAP, school readiness, assessment practices, and national and state legislative actions.

## *Develop On-Going Parent Education and Involvement Projects*

Because DAP is unfamiliar to most parents and community members, it must be clearly explained. The committee should develop a plan for parent education and parent involvement. Teachers need to be freed to spend a considerable amount of time educating parents about the use of learning centers, projects, and the whole language philosophy. Classroom visits and volunteer work are essential in convincing parents that well-implemented, concrete learning experiences encourage children to enjoy school, relate better to each other, and become effective thinkers. Parental involvement has been an important element for many schools which switched from a traditional curriculum to a DAP format. The committee should consider the following strategies for educating and involving parents and other members of the community:

**Organize an active parent involvement/education program.** This could include orientations, meetings, open houses and parent-teacher conferences to provide opportunities for DAP to be explained. Show slides and video tapes of children engaged in age-appropriate activities. Create parents' bulletin boards to display articles and pictures related to DAP.

**Plan mini-parent libraries within each school.** These can contain books, reprinted articles and audio/video cassettes which are easily loaned to parents. Appendix D contains a list of suggested titles.

**Seek grant money for a speaker series.** Then video-tape each speaker and place the tapes on loan in the library. Create a public relations sub-committee to assist parents in understanding the benefits of high-quality early childhood curriculum practices. The sub-committee can write articles for local newspapers, arrange interviews for radio and television, and write letters to the editor. Make a special public relations effort during the "Week of the Young Child" in April.

**Distribute booklets and posters about DAP to all parents and board members.** Purchase inexpensive posters such as "Children Learn Mathematics Through Active Exploration," and booklets such as "Good Teaching Practices for 4 and 5 Year-olds" and "Appropriate Education in the Primary Grades" from NAEYC.

**Read NAEYC 's *Developmentally Appropriate Practices*, Part 8, which is entitled "Informing Others About DAP."** This contains many specific suggestions for educating the community about the importance of developmentally appropriate practices.

## *Support Teacher Education and Recognition*

**Provide DAP in-service workshops for teachers.** Topics should include: how to respond to wide variability in 4 through 8 year-olds, developing and managing learning centers, the whole language approach to teaching reading and writing, children's literature throughout the curriculum, and manipulative math and science.

**Acquire and utilize the High Scope Materials.** *Young Children in Action: A Manual for Pre-School Educators* and *The Cognitively Oriented Curriculum* (Elementary Education Series) are creative manuals that provide excellent information on child-initiated activities. They are also exemplary source materials for the in-service workshops.

**Encourage teachers to enroll in graduate courses involving a study of DAP.** Requirements for completion of these courses often involves action research. As part of their courses, teachers can write proposals specifying how they would redesign their curriculums to become more age-appropriate.

**Encourage teachers to invite administrators, board members and parents to observe and participate in their classrooms as the classes become more and more developmentally appropriate.** The teachers should describe the specific skills and concepts being learned as the children interact with concrete and meaningful materials.

## *Conduct On-Going Curriculum Evaluation*

The primary goal of the Early Childhood Education committee is to begin a full-year study of the kindergarten curriculum, followed by a study of the first grade curriculum during the second year, and the second and third grade curriculums during the third and fourth years.

**Evaluate current curriculum practices by comparing them with the guidelines described in the NAEYC's *Developmentally Appropriate Practice: Early Childhood Programs Serving Children from Birth Through Age Eight,* and *A Notebook For Teachers: Making Changes In the Elementary Curriculum,* written by Robert Wood and members of the Northeast Foundation for Children.** Both books provide research-based information on developmentally effective teaching methods and learning experiences.

**Investigate new materials and classroom management techniques in each subject area.** Obtain whole language reading materials from The Wright Group, Rigby, and Scholastic Inc. Other whole language materials are available from Modern Learning Press, the publisher of this book. A good manipulative math program for K-12, ***Math Their Way,*** has been published by Addison-Wesley. In the area of science, ***The Elementary Science Program Study Curriculum,*** developed by Educational Development Center (EDC), contains over 50 units in discovery science.

## *Examine Your School's Written Philosophy*

Robert Johnson, formerly an elementary school principal in Chesterfield, New Hampshire, believes that a school's stated philosophy should be closely related to what actually happens in classrooms. Notice how his school's philosophy, quoted below, provides a strong rationale for teaching methods and learning experiences which are consistent with the learning characteristics of children through the age of 8.

"Educational experiences for elementary-aged children at Chesterfield Elementary School:

are based on the understanding that young children learn through play, concrete experiences, and other non-traditional academic activities, materials and environments;

are oriented to individual developmental patterns and varied learning styles;

emphasize interrelationships among reading, language arts, and other areas of the curriculum;

emphasize expansion of experiences: language development, listening and thinking skills, social-emotional development, and perceptual motor abilities;

reflect the fact that a child's positive self-concept is an essential ingredient for learning;

reflect concerns of parents and community for quality programs but also help parents understand the multidimensional needs of young learners from various cultures and environments;

The Chesterfield philosophy emphasizes allowing the child to grow and develop on nature's timeline and letting readiness emerge. It encourages experiences through which children can make discoveries about things, about life, about themselves. It advocates acceptance of children without condition and with respect for the unique human beings they are."

**Determine whether your school's philosophy is consistent with current teaching practices. If not, it should be rewritten to reflect child development knowledge.**

Designing a curriculum which is based on child development knowledge is a major step in helping young children become better learners, but it is only half of the change process. The other half is determining appropriate ways to evaluate children's learning. School administrators are expected to clearly demonstrate that children are learning satisfactorily. State departments of education and local boards of education often require these administrators to evaluate achievement through the use of standardized, group-administered tests. In the primary grades, these tests result in inappropriate practices, because their adoption pressures teachers to cover material in a way that results in high scores but little real learning.

Chapter 6 describes several alternative evaluation procedures that are consistent with a developmentally appropriate approach to teaching. Like the DAP curriculum, they engender self-esteem, curiosity, creativity, and a positive attitude toward learning.

*Practice* 6

# Support alternatives to standardized achievement tests

| | |
|---|---|
| Teacher Observation | ✔ |
| Behavior Checklist | ✔ |
| Writing Samples | ✔ |
| Reading Lists | ✔ |
| Art Work Portfolio | ✔ |

*During the fourth week of kindergarten, Cheryl and her classmates were given a standardized achievement test. The teacher verbally conveyed the test questions to the children and asked them to "fill in the bubble" under the picture showing the correct answer on their test sheets. With a #2 pencil in hand, Cheryl nervously filled in each "bubble" representing the answer she thought was right. However, when Cheryl's teacher said, "Find the picture of the horse running," Cheryl thought to herself "Horses don't run; they gallop." She did not answer that question or several others she found confusing. Cheryl's level of anxiety increased during the week, as small portions of the test were completed each day. Some students cried. One child vomited. Many felt frustrated and fatigued.*

*A few weeks later, Cheryl's parents received a computerized sheet reporting a low score and recommending her for basic skill instruction. Also, they were told that the results of the test determined that Cheryl would be placed into the low reading group. Her parents were devastated. How could such a bright child, who loved to learn and who had blossomed in preschool, do so poorly on a test? What went wrong?*

To be sure, nothing is wrong with Cheryl. She is simply a victim of an inappropriate assessment. Like many students across America, Cheryl has been narrowly and unfairly judged by a single test score, which is regarded as the definitive evidence of her learning achievements and ability. Like all young children, her learning process is much too dynamic to rely upon a single measure of any device, especially a standardized, group-administered achievement test.

## Standardized Tests

The main purpose of standardized tests is to compare the achievement of groups of students, and to provide a basis for charting trends over time. In addition, however, such tests have been used to place students in learning groups or grade levels, to assess teacher performance, and to establish accountability standards for school districts.

While standardized tests are rarely used to grade students on their classroom performance, they often have a profound effect on what happens in the classroom. In a study called "Testing In Kindergarten," Dr. Dolores Durkin, Professor of Education at Rutgers University, found that teachers seldom use standardized test results to change instruction to suit individual children's needs. Instead, teachers have been found to respond to test results by trying to teach all the children the same test-related content using the same methods. The end result is often a primary school classroom which has become a "cram course," utilizing developmentally inappropriate teaching methods and emphasizing concepts that many young children are not yet capable of understanding.

A first grade teacher I know felt pressured to teach the concept of time to her children, because they would be administered a standardized achievement test containing "time items." She first taught time by using a large cardboard clock with movable hands. Then she passed out worksheets with pictures of clocks showing different times, and the children had to "fill in" the correct answer underneath each item. When I asked her if the children understood what they were doing, the teacher replied, "Only the 'high group' understands!"

Her comment supports studies cited in Carol Seefeldt's book, ***Social Studies for the Preschool-Primary Child.*** Seefeldt, director of the Institute for Child Study at the University of Maryland, concludes that by age 5 most children can determine what day it is, but it is not until age 7 that they are able to tell time in a conventional manner. It is developmentally appropriate, therefore, to begin teaching time in a formal manner in the second grade, but not before.

The tests themselves have similar limitations in regard to children's development. Clearly, such tests are only appropriate when children have developed test-taking and logical thinking skills needed to generate an accurate and reliable score. In most children, such skills are evident at the end of the third grade or beginning of the fourth grade. Only at that time, but not before, standardized tests can play a role in ensuring that children's learning is objectively assessed.

Another concern about standardized tests is that they measure national reading objectives, not local instructional goals. And, the National Association for the Education of Young Children (NAEYC), in its document entitled "NAEYC Position Statement on Standardized Testing of Young Children 3 Through 8 Years of Age," argues that these tests "frequently do not reflect current theory and research about how young children learn." For example, current research on reading instruction supports a whole language philosophy that integrates oral language, writing, reading, and spelling in meaningful contexts, with an emphasis on comprehension. Standardized tests, however, are concerned with measuring knowledge of isolated skills. The use of these tests below the third grade encourages teachers to teach reading without creating a meaningful context, just so that their students will score well on the tests.

These and other problems associated with the use of standardized, group-administered achievement tests are explored further in the pages that follow.

## *Insensitivity to Developmental Characteristics*

Standardized tests are not sensitive to young children's unique developmental characteristics. Lawrence Schweinhart, a researcher for the High/Scope Educational Research Foundation and author of ***A School Administrator's Guide To Early Childhood Programs,*** states that such tests are "wholly inappropriate for young children in content, format, and the sustained attention that they require of children."

More specifically, standardized tests cannot accurately measure young children's emerging skills and understanding of concepts, because primary-age students are not good test takers. Many of them do not yet understand the test directions, nor are they ready for the abstract, paper-and-pencil-type tasks. They may just be starting to comprehend school-related concepts such as "test," "sentence," "numeral," "plus," and "minus." Test makers assume children come to school understanding these words, but many do not. It takes time and repeated exposures to concepts before children develop an accurate conceptual framework.

Standardized tests also pose a risk of psychological harm at a time when young children are adjusting to new people, unfamiliar surroundings, and new terminology. They are placed under additional stress when seating arrangements are changed in preparation for the test. And, this is compounded by the abrupt change in the teacher's role from "helper" to "tester," unable to be of assistance in providing answers. Tom Schultz, author of "Testing and Retention of Young Children," criticizes standardized tests because they create undue stress that is harmful to the development of positive attitudes toward school.

Furthermore, standardized tests emphasize learning goals which are not necessarily the most important goals of early childhood education. Dr. Lillian Katz, author of the article, "Dispositions In Early Childhood Education," says that many critically important ability and attitudinal areas -- such as developing self-esteem, social competence, creativity, and dispositions toward learning -- are considered unmeasurable and therefore eliminated from tests. Tests in the early grades address easy-to-assess areas such as reading and arithmetic skills. However, that does not mean these skills are more important than those abilities that are not easily appraised. The tendency to remedy educational ills by embracing a "psychometric" testing model is all too pervasive. Although access to quantified data may appear reassuring, it is actually a superficial comfort. We must question the assumption that abilities are more valuable when they are measurable.

## *Premature Labeling*

Another problem with standardized tests has to do with the premature labeling that they often encourage. Students may be identified as lacking "basic skills" or placed into the "low" reading group on the basis of a single test score that may not reflect true ability. Such practices discriminate against late maturing children who consolidate their cognitive, visual and small-muscle skills at a different age than what standardized test criteria deem the "norm."

The stigma of receiving an early label can produce feelings of inadequacy in both children and their parents. Early identification may have a negative effect upon a child's entire course of development. Anxieties are heightened and expectations from teachers and parents are lowered; this in turn can have a negative influence on the way children are treated in school and at home. It can also result in children developing negative attitudes toward school and themselves.

Accurate assessment methods can help to identify young children who truly need remedial instruction. Yet, this may result in children being sent out of the classroom, often for 30 minutes of basic skills instruction three times a week, which creates related labeling problems. From a developmental point of view, such "pull-out" programs in the primary grades are ineffective and frustrating because they violate children's social needs to "belong" -- to feel like part of the group and not be seen as different from others. Does it make sense, for example, to remove children several times a week from a half-day kindergarten, especially when they are likely to miss playtime, the high point of the day? If children are found to need special help, instruction should be provided within the classroom, in an unobtrusive and non-stigmatizing manner.

## *Cultural Bias*

Standardized tests contain culture-specific test items. These items may be unfamiliar to culturally different children who have adequate skills and demonstrate an understanding of concepts within culturally familiar settings. The NAEYC's position statement on testing recommends that standardized tests not be used in multicultural and multilingual communities, if the tests are not sensitive to the effects of cultural diversity or bilingualism. At the very least, bilingual children should be tested in their parents' language as well as in the English language.

## *Teaching to The Test*

Many teachers find themselves in a difficult dilemma. Their performance is often evaluated, in part, by the results of their student test scores. This places them under a great deal of pressure not only to gear their instruction directly to the content on the test, but also to present materials in a similar format to the test. In effect, the test publishers become the curriculum directors for the school system.

"Teaching to the test" in a primary grade classroom results in misguided priorities. Excessive amounts of precious class time are used for test preparation. The NAEYC brochure entitled "Testing of Young Children" describes how a primary grade teacher, under pressure to improve achievement test scores, eliminates learning centers, outdoor play, music and art activities, in order to increase time for "daily phonics drills."

Anyone can teach to a test! It takes little skill, creativity, or talent. Yet, young children learn best when teachers generate excitement for learning and motivate students to want to read, write, and enjoy math. When teachers of young children are pressured to teach to a test, their opportunities to motivate children are severely hampered. A boring, abstract curriculum is created, because students are taught to care most about correct answers and are not challenged to think and be imaginative. This can also lead young children to develop negative attitudes about school and themselves, because their natural inclination to learn in meaningful ways is thwarted.

# Alternatives to Standardized Tests

Alternative assessment methods that fairly and accurately evaluate young children are an intrinsic part of a curriculum based on developmentally appropriate practices. In the report, ***Right From The Start***, the National Association of State Boards of Education recommends "that states should support the development of alternatives to standardized tests for young children." The use of alternatives is already spreading across America as part of the movement to implement developmentally appropriate practices.

Anne Stallman and David Pearson, directors of the Center for the Study of Reading at the University of Illinois, have intensively studied the assessment of young students. They have concluded that the most accurate methods of evaluating the learning of young children, especially in literacy development, involves conducting individual assessments of children while they are engaged in meaningful classroom activity. Such assessments focus on student performance of tasks, with teacher observation, checklists, and individual student portfolios being used to evaluate peformance. These techniques allow teachers to make on-going "situational" judgments of student progress.

## *Informal Teacher Observation*

Informal observation, regarded by most educators as vital to the evaluation of children's learning, occurs as teachers move about the classroom. It involves gathering data by watching children attentively and then interpreting what the information means. Many teachers, however, do not do this in a systematic way because they are too busy completing the many teaching tasks required during a school day. It is necessary, therefore, to schedule time for observation and recording of children's behaviors. A kindergarten teacher I know was able to observe more efficiently by setting aside five minutes each day to observe her students. She wore a sign that said "observer," and the children knew they were not allowed to speak to her during those five minutes. She was surprised at how much information she was able to obtain in such a short period of time.

While moving around the classroom during an informal observation, the teacher watches and listens to students engaged in individual or group activities. Notebooks, index cards and pencils can be placed in strategic positions around the room, so that notes about the children's behaviors can be recorded easily. Kindergarten teacher Wendy Hood, in an article entitled "If The Teacher Comes Over, Pretend It's A Telescope," explains how she closely observed her students' varied levels of development, especially as to their fine motor skills. She notes, for example, that children new to the use of scissors tend to open and close their jaws as they open and close the scissors. Experienced cutters show no jaw or mouth movement related to cutting. According to Millie Almy and Celia Genishi, authors of ***Ways of Studying Children***, this attention to detail provides clues to the meaning of behavior.

Teachers can improve their observational skills by reading their book and ***The Classroom Observer*** by Dr. Ann Boehm. And, when they observe students on a regular basis during the school year, teachers can compile information needed to discuss each child knowledgably with parents and prepare year-end reports on student achievement.

## *Formal Observation*

Formal observation involves the use of specific anecdotal records such as observation forms and checklists. Observation forms used to assess young children's reading abilities have been developed by Edward Chittenden, research psychologist for the Educational Testing Service. These forms are available in his article, "Assessment of Young Children's Reading: Documentation as an Alternative." Chittenden recommends that teachers focus on "story time" and "choice time" as particularly good settings for observation.

Significant assessment information is obtained during "story time" by reading aloud to children and listening to their responses to questions. Following the story, the richness of individual students' vocabulary, knowledge of story structures, and ability to predict are recorded on forms. Also, they may be asked to retell a story and identify the main idea, which reveals important information about their abilities to remember and summarize. The way they participate in follow-up discussions provides information about their ability to ask relevant questions, which is also recorded on the forms.

During "choice time," teachers take note of which books and activities are chosen by children. Do they choose books the teacher or classmates have read? Or do they choose books that have a unique appeal to them alone? Do they closely study the text of a book or look only at the pictures? Do they turn the pages sequentially? Are they able to work cooperatively? Is there a relationship between their social skills and their ability to learn? When recorded on forms, the answers to these questions provide important information about the child's unique learning patterns and progress.

Dr. Margaret Lay-Dopyera, Professor at Syracuse University, has developed a kindergarten observation assessment form called "Report". The teacher or aide observes individual children during informal classroom settings and responds in writing to a series of questions. Lay-Dopyera suggests that the ground rule for using "Report" is that "evidence collected for addressing the questions must come from observations of spontaneous behavior, not testing, interviewing, or contrived task situations." Here are some examples of the questions:

"Under what circumstances and in what ways does the child evidence an interest in knowing about the messages encoded in print (hearing stories read, hearing letters read, reading signs, following directions)?"

"To what extent does the child's own writing approximate standard writing practices (e.g., left to right, top to bottom, use of letter forms in writing, combinations of letters to form words, extent of letter-sound correspondence, sentence formation, paragraph formation)?"

"What evidence is there that the child has heard what adults and other children say?"

"What are examples of the child's counting ability?"

As with informal observation, the use of observation forms throughout the year provides detailed information for parent conferences and year-end reports.

## *Checklists*

Checklists may be employed at any age or grade level. They are used to evaluate each child's level of skill and concept development in relation to a set of locally determined curriculum goals. A child's reading and math progress, for example, can be assessed by transferring anecdotal information to a checklist containing items such as the sample kindergarten checklist items below. The teacher places a check mark under the appropriate column, and provides the date and any comment regarding new progress. This information, gathered over a period of weeks or months, is used to design appropriate learning experiences that support children's ongoing development.

| | Most of Time | Some of Time | Not At All | Date |
|---|---|---|---|---|
| Understands that print carries meaning | | | | |
| Understands concepts of "letter" and "word" | | | | |
| Enjoys listening to stories | | | | |
| Interested in writing letters in own name | | | | |
| Recalls and retells a story in complete sentences | | | | |
| Recognizes words beginning with same sound | | | | |
| Uses pencil or crayon with control | | | | |
| Writes numerals 1-10 | | | | |

Comments:

A checklist can be easily misused, however, especially when teachers lack training in child development. Following are guidelines for their proper use:

The results of a checklist allow teachers to create activities that move children to the next step. The checklist should not be regarded as a test used to label children.

The wide individual variation in young children's developmental abilities and their unpredictable rate of growth must be respected and accepted. Therefore, it is unrealistic and unfair to expect all the children in a specific age group or grade level to progress according to a predetermined schedule.

Teachers provide parents with information about children's progress based on the goals achieved. They should not create undue parental anxiety by emphasizing deficits and identifying goals that have not been reached.

As with observation forms, information from a checklist is gathered by teachers or aides during natural -- not contrived --classroom interactions. The information is used by teachers to design developmentally appropriate experiences and not to teach isolated skills in an abstract or formal manner.

The importance of the checklist should not be exaggerated. It is a tool used within the curriculum but is not the essence of the curriculum. The stated items are less important than goals such as well-rounded development, self-esteem, curiosity, and a positive attitude toward learning.

There are several resources containing well-researched checklists. My own three-volume set of books entitled ***Preschool Curriculum Library,*** written with Kathleen Coletta, contains checklists for 2, 3, and 4 year-old children. ***Literacy Development In the Early Years: Helping Children Read and Write,*** by Lesley Mandel Morrow, contains checklists regarding children's concepts about books, print, and ability to understand story structure.

Keep in mind, however, that checklists are "criterion-referenced," as opposed to the "norm-referenced" instruments which were described in Chapter 4. This means they do not compare children with others, but instead reflect each child's degree of mastery over a sequence of skills and concepts deemed important by educators. Therefore, a checklist should be developed or modified by classroom teachers and those skilled in the areas of assessment and child development, in order to be consistent with specific curriculums and groups of children.

## *Portfolios of Children's Work*

A portfolio is a folder of assessment materials collected over time. It can include writing samples, tape recordings of students reading stories aloud, lists of books students have read, artwork, and interviews with students. The portfolio is used to document student competence and levels of performance in all areas of development.

The work actually produced by children often can be used as tangible evidence of learning. Writing samples that are collected every two to four weeks can furnish clear documentation of improvement over time in language and handwriting skills, as well as organized thinking. In their article, "Writing Development In Early Childhood," Elizabeth Sulzby and William Teale conclude that information from portfolios -- such as young children's progress from writing letters to writing words -- can help predict their growth toward reading.

Teachers can also be trained to keep "running records" of oral reading as a way of assessing the strategies students are using to read. These written records identify which words are misread and note when a child is attempting to invent text. Also, a student's word omissions, repetitions, substitutions, and self-corrections can be noted. Procedures for completing a "running record" can be found in ***The Early Detection of Reading Difficulties*** by Marie Clay, and in Appendix F of Regie Routman's book, ***Transitions: From Literature to Literacy.***

## *Utilizing Appropriate Assessment Information*

The evidence collected through observation and checklists, combined with samples of students' work, provides a truer picture of children's performance than standardized achievement test scores. I also believe that enlightened teacher observation better identifies children who need remedial or basic-skills instruction, and provides a sound foundation for modifications in the curriculum.

This opinion is supported by an article entitled "Forget The Test, The Teacher Knows Best," which was published in ***The American Teacher.*** In the article, the California State Education Department reports that kindergarten teachers' judgments were found to be a better indicator of children's potential reading problems than standardized tests designed to identify these deficiencies.

By utilizing observation, checklists and portfolios, teachers and parents can determine on a local level how well young children are learning. Comparisons of students on a statewide or national level prior to third grade require the use of standardized achievement tests, and are therefore very likely to be inaccurate and damaging.

Alternative assessments can also be used to grade students on the progress they have made during the school year. Report cards can be narratives or modified checklists, rather than letter or numeral grades. The latter grading systems can have a negative impact on young children's self-esteem, unfairly penalize late bloomers, and create an atmosphere of competition rather than cooperative learning.

Teachers of young children can certainly increase the validity of their judgments by continually improving their observation skills and expanding their knowledge of how young children learn to read, write, speak, and compute. But it makes perfect sense that those who work with a group of children day in and day out are in the best position to assess students' strengths and weaknesses.

## Strategies to Support Alternatives to Standardized Achievement Tests

The unique developmental needs of young children require teachers and parents to advocate the use of developmentally appropriate assessment techniques, instead of standardized achievement tests. Some states have already taken steps to provide more appropriate assessments. North Carolina has postponed the use of standardized testing until third grade, when children are better able to cope with tests, and the results are therefore more reliable. California no longer requires standardized testing in kindergarten and first grade. Similar changes have occurred in Texas, Arizona, and Mississippi. The following strategies can help teachers and parents working in partnership make sure that young children are assessed appropriately.

**Distribute information to all members of the community on alternative assessment strategies and the dangers of using standardized tests with young children.** Providing information from authoritative sources to educators, parents, and school board members is particularly important. See ***Achievement Testing in the Early Grades: The Games Grownups Play,*** co-edited by Constance Kamii, which is a collection of articles by early childhood experts who have called for a halt to achievement testing in grades K-2. Also see the May, 1989 issue of ***Phi Delta Kappan,*** the April, 1989 issue of ***Educational Leadership,*** and the NAEYC's ***Guidelines for Appropriate Curriculum Content and Assessment.***

**Encourage school administrators, board members and state department of education officials to support the use of developmentally appropriate assessment procedures.** These include more reliance on trained teacher observation and student work samples, combined with less reliance on standardized tests. Invite parents and board members into the classroom to view how teachers document signs of student progress without reliance on standardized tests.

**Contact the National Center for Fair and Open Testing (Fairtest) in Cambridge, Massachusetts.** They will assist groups in their political and legal efforts to eliminate standardized testing in the primary grades.

**Support teacher in-service courses in alternative assessment techniques.** Studies have indicated that most teachers need additional training in skillful observation and use of forms and checklists. And, teachers feel empowered when they are involved in the development of alternative assessments and trained in their use.

**Make use of books that can help teachers develop alternative assessments.** Marie Clay's ***What Did I Write?*** describes ways teachers can examine students' writing samples. ***Writing: Teachers and Children At Work,*** by Donald Graves, outlines stages of invented spelling which can be used in assessing children's writing development. ***The Primary Language Record,*** published by Heinemann Educational Books, contains forms for collecting and evaluating children's writing and reading samples. Work in mathematics can be assessed in the primary grades with the ***Mathematics Their Way*** program, written by Mary Baratta Lorton.

United action by parents and teachers can provide a powerful impetus to create policies that are based on knowledge of how children grow and develop. The following appendices are designed to help readers of this book take further action to do what's best for kids.

# Kindergarten Readiness Checklist For Parents

*After reading each question below, respond by circling the number that best applies to each question. The questions are worded so that the "some of the time" and "not at this time" responses indicate readiness.*

*Pay particular attention to questions receiving a "most of the time" answer, especially if the child will turn 5 years-old between June and the school's cutoff date. As these answers indicate the child may not be ready for kindergarten, the areas of concern that are identified will be important factors in making a decision about kindergarten entrance. Information from the child's preschool teacher(s), the advice or primary school personnel, and the results of assessments should also be included in the decision-making process.*

| | Most of the time | Some of the time | Not at this time |
|---|---|---|---|
| EMOTIONAL MATURITY -- Does the child: | | | |
| 1. Show a lack of confidence when engaged in learning activities? | 3 | 2 | 1 |
| 2. Cry or have temper tantrums when things don't go his/her way? | 3 | 2 | 1 |
| 3. Get upset when separated from Mom or Dad? | 3 | 2 | 1 |

| | Most of the time | Some of the time | Not at this time |
|---|---|---|---|
| 4. Seem worried or nervous? | 3 | 2 | 1 |
| 5. Appear timid or fearful? | 3 | 2 | 1 |
| 6. Get easily frustrated by tasks? | 3 | 2 | 1 |
| SOCIAL MATURITY -- Does the child: | | | |
| 7. Have difficulty playing cooperatively with other children? | 3 | 2 | 1 |
| 8. Prefer to play with younger playmates? | 3 | 2 | 1 |
| 9. Have difficulty sharing toys or food, or taking turns with playmates? | 3 | 2 | 1 |
| 10. Behave in a shy manner and avoid making contact with other children? | 3 | 2 | 1 |
| 11. Appear overwhelmed by peers of the same age? | 3 | 2 | 1 |

| | Most of the time | Some of the time | Not at this time |
|---|---|---|---|
| PHYSICAL MATURITY -- Does the child: | | | |
| 12. Have trouble sitting still, listening, and/or persisting with an adult-directed task for 15 minutes or longer? | 3 | 2 | 1 |
| 13. Have difficulty grasping a pencil comfortably and close to the point? | 3 | 2 | 1 |
| 14. Show little or no interest in focusing on a letter or word? | 3 | 2 | 1 |
| 15. Walk or run in a clumsy, awkward manner? | 3 | 2 | 1 |
| 16. Have difficulty skipping or hopping on one foot? | 3 | 2 | 1 |
| 17. Have difficulty throwing and catching a large ball? | 3 | 2 | 1 |
| 18. Appear to be smaller than children of the same age? | 3 | 2 | 1 |

| | Most of the time | Some of the time | Not at this time |
|---|---|---|---|
| INTELLECTUAL MATURITY -- Does the child: | | | |
| 19. Show a lack of interest in books? | 3 | 2 | 1 |
| 20. Seldom ask to be read to? | 3 | 2 | 1 |
| 21. Have problems recalling past events, or words to songs and rhymes? | 3 | 2 | 1 |
| 22. Have difficulty identifying and remembering common objects such as cars, plants, airplanes, etc.? | 3 | 2 | 1 |
| 23. Struggle to understand concepts such as colors, letters, numbers, and shapes? | 3 | 2 | 1 |
| 24. Have difficulty saying common words, such as saying "firsty" instead of "thirsty?" | 3 | 2 | 1 |
| 25. Have difficulty following two or more directions? | 3 | 2 | 1 |
| 26. Have difficulty describing how simple objects are used? | 3 | 2 | 1 |

# Informal Teacher Observation Checklist For 4 And 5 Year-Olds

*The following informal checklist can be used by teachers to gather information about the social and emotional maturity of 4 and 5 year-olds.*

*To utilize this checklist, circle the number indicating the type of behavior observed. A "3" indicates more positive behavior, a "2" indicates neutral behavior, and a "1" indicates more negative behavior.*

*If a "1" is frequently circled, the child may be in need of additional help with social and emotional development.*

| | | | | |
|---|---|---|---|---|
| Responds to directions | 3 | 2 | 1 | Refuses to cooperate |
| Focuses on a task | 3 | 2 | 1 | Is distracted |
| Sits still and attends | 3 | 2 | 1 | Is constantly in motion |
| Is sociable, outgoing | 3 | 2 | 1 | Is shy, fearful |
| Persists with a task | 3 | 2 | 1 | Gives up easily |
| Separates easily | 3 | 2 | 1 | Has problems separating |
| Speaks understandably | 3 | 2 | 1 | Speech is unclear |
| Uses complete sentences | 3 | 2 | 1 | Speaks in single words |

# DAP Checklist for Teacher and Parent Behavior

*Proactive teaching and parenting is needed when making decisions which are healthy for children. Such adult leadership is informed, active, and developmentally appropriate.*

*How can you determine the extent to which your teaching or parenting behaviors are developmentally appropriate? Complete the checklist below by circling a number that best describes your situation.*

*1 = does not occur at this time*
*2 = occurs some of the time*
*3 = occurs most of the time*
*4 = always occurs (close to 100% of the time)*

*A score of between 30 and 40 on either the school or home scales indicates developmentally appropriate teaching or parenting. A score between 20 and 29 suggests that the adult behaviors are more inappropriate than appropriate. A score under 20 indicates extensive inappropriate practices.*

## School

| | Always | Most of the time | Some of the time | Not At this time |
|---|---|---|---|---|
| 1. Children are involved with concrete materials related to their life experiences, and have minimal involvement with worksheets and workbooks. | 4 | 3 | 2 | 1 |

| | Always | Most of the time | Some of the time | Not At this time |
|---|---|---|---|---|
| 2. Different levels of ability and development are expected, respected, and responded to by the teacher. | 4 | 3 | 2 | 1 |
| 3. Children are allowed to learn at their own pace while acquiring reading, writing, and math skills. | 4 | 3 | 2 | 1 |
| 4. Learning occurs primarily through learning centers and small group projects in all traditional subject areas. | 4 | 3 | 2 | 1 |
| 5. Reading and writing are taught through an emerging literacy approach: storybook reading, writing centers, language experience, and dramatic play. | 4 | 3 | 2 | 1 |
| 6. Many mathematical manipulative materials are provided, and science projects encourage exploration and active involvement. | 4 | 3 | 2 | 1 |

| | Always | Most of the time | Some of the time | Not At this time |
|---|---|---|---|---|
| 7. Art, music, and movement are integrated throughout the curriculum each day. | 4 | 3 | 2 | 1 |
| 8. Outdoor activity is regularly and frequently scheduled. | 4 | 3 | 2 | 1 |
| 9. Discipline consists of setting and enforcing clear limits in a positive manner, redirecting children to an acceptable activity, and involving children in establishing rules. | 4 | 3 | 2 | 1 |
| 10. Children's achievement is evaluated through the use of teacher observation (anecdotal records and checklists) and performance samples, not standardized achievement tests. | 4 | 3 | 2 | 1 |

**Home**

| | | | | |
|---|---|---|---|---|
| 1. Adults pay as much attention to social, emotional, and physical aspects of children's development, as they do to the intellectual aspect. | 4 | 3 | 2 | 1 |

| | Always | Most of the time | Some of the time | Not At this time |
|---|---|---|---|---|
| 2. Parents see themselves as confident leaders who balance an abundance of love with fun and clearly stated limits. | 4 | 3 | 2 | 1 |
| 3. Parents work actively and cooperatively with the school to assess the readiness of the child to enter kindergarten. | 4 | 3 | 2 | 1 |
| 4. Parents support the child's involvement in physical activities, but avoid placing him or her in organized, highly competitive sports until the child is physically and emotionally ready for such activities. | 4 | 3 | 2 | 1 |
| 5. Parents see each child as a unique individual. They do not use siblings to make comparisons which can lead to rivalry and insecurity. | 4 | 3 | 2 | 1 |
| 6. Children receive frequent praise and affection from parents. | 4 | 3 | 2 | 1 |

| | Always | Most of the time | Some of the time | Not At this time |
|---|---|---|---|---|
| 7. Parents take time to engage in activities with children and not just direct the activities. | 4 | 3 | 2 | 1 |
| 8. The amount of television children watch is carefully monitored. Parents make sure young children are not allowed to view shows containing sex and violence. | 4 | 3 | 2 | 1 |
| 9. Children are encouraged to express themselves verbally and use relaxation responses (such as deep breathing) in stressful situations. | 4 | 3 | 2 | 1 |
| 10. Parents place children in nursery schools that are play-oriented rather than academically oriented. | 4 | 3 | 2 | 1 |

# References and Resources for Developmentally Appropriate Practices

*The materials listed in this appendix can be used by teachers and parents to promote developmentally appropriate decision making in their schools and homes. Bibliographic information is provided for each of the authors, books and journal articles referred to in the Introduction and Chapters 1 through 6. Also included, starting with Chapter 1, is a list of additional books and articles, audiovisual materials, and organizations pertinent to various topics discussed in the Chapter. Most of these references and resources can be easily obtained from local libraries or by writing to the publisher.*

*Teachers and parents can focus their efforts to change inappropriate policies by following an easy-to-remember "ABCD" course of action:*

*A -- Accumulate relevant books and articles on developmentally appropriate practices.*

*B -- Believe in the principle that the education and guidance of young children should be based on what is known about how they learn and develop.*

*C -- Connect with other teachers and parents in supporting and organizing programs emphasizing a developmental approach.*

*D -- Disseminate articles, brochures, books and audiovisual materials through school libraries and parent/teacher organizations.*

# Foreword

## *References*

Boyer, Ernest. "What Teachers Say About Children in America." ***Educational Leadership***, Vol. 46. No. 8, May, 1989.

Egan, James. Keynote speech to teachers, Fair Lawn, NJ, October 19, 1988.

# Introduction

## *References*

Balaban, Nancy. "Balancing Priorities for Children." A keynote address presented at the Oregon Joint Conference on Early Childhood Education, March 7, 1987. ERIC document: 280 599.

Cherry, Clare, et al. ***Is The Left Brain Always Right?*** Belmont, CA: David Lake Publishers, 1989.

Dopyera, John, and Lay-Dopyera, Margaret. ***Becoming a Teacher of Young Children***. New York: McGraw-Hill, 1990.

Dobson, James. ***The Strong-Willed Child: Birth Through Adolescence***. Wheaton, IL: Tyndale House, 1988.

Elkind, David. ***The Hurried Child: Growing Up Too Fast Too Soon***. Reading, MA: Addison-Wesley, 1981.

"NAEYC Position Statement on Developmentally Appropriate Practice in the Primary Grades Serving 5- Through 8-Year-Olds (Part 7)." In Sue Bredekamp (Ed.), ***Developmentally Appropriate Practice in Early Childhood Programs Serving Children From Birth Through Age 8***. Washington, DC: National Association for the Education of Young Children, 1987.

Putka, Gary. "Tense Tots: Some Schools Press So Hard Kids Become Stressed and Fearful." ***The Wall Street Journal***, July 6, 1988.

Roby, Pamela. ***Child Care — Who Cares? Foreign and Domestic Infant and Early Childhood Development Policies***. New York: Basic Books, 1973.

Soderman, Anne, and Phillips, Marian. "The Early Education of Males: Where Are We Failing Them?" ***Educational Leadership***, November, 1986.

Spock, Benjamin. ***Baby and Child Care.*** New York: Hawthorn Books, 1968.

Spock, Benjamin. "Don't Push Your Kids Too Hard." ***U.S. News and World Report***, October 27, 1986.

Tanner, James. ***Foetus Into Man: Physical Growth From Conception to Maturity.*** Cambridge, MA: Harvard University Press, 1978.

Thomas, Alexander, and Chess, Stella. ***Temperament and Development.*** New York: Brunner/Mazel, 1977.

Turecki, Stanley, and Leslie Tonner. ***The Difficult Child.*** New York: Bantam Books, 1985.

Winn, Marie. ***Children Without Childhood.*** New York: Plenum, 1983.

Zigler, Edward, and Lang, Mary. "The Emergence of 'Superbaby': A Good Thing?" ***Pediatric Nursing***, Vol. 11, Sept./Oct., 1985.

# Chapter 1

## *References*

Ames, Louise Bates. ***Is Your Child in the Wrong Grade?*** New York: Harper and Row, 1967.

Apell, Richard. ***Preschool Vision.*** St. Louis: American Optometry Association, 1959.

Bronfenbrenner, Urie. ***Two Worlds of Childhood: U.S. and U.S.S.R.*** New York: Pocket Books, 1973.

Dobson, James. ***Hide or Seek.*** Old Tappan, NJ: Fleming H. Revell, 1979.

Elkind, David. ***Miseducation: Preschoolers At Risk.*** New York: Alfred Knopf, 1987.

Erikson, Erik. ***Childhood and Society***. New York: Norton, 1963.

Faber, Adele, and Mazlish, Elaine. ***How To Talk So Kids Will Listen & Listen So Kids Will Talk***. New York: Rawson, Wade, 1980.

Fluegelman, Andrew. ***The New Games Book***. Garden City, NY: Dolphin Books, 1976.

Gray, Lillian. ***Teaching Children to Read***. New York: The Ronald Press Co., 1963.

Hilliard, Asa. "How Should We Assess Children's Social Competence?" ***Young Children***, Vol. 33, No. 5, July, 1978.

Honig, Alice Sterling. "The Shy Child." ***Young Children***, Vol. 42, No. 4, May, 1987.

Hyson, Marion, and van Trieste, Karen. ***The Shy Child***. Urbana, IL. ERIC Clearinghouse on Elementary and Early Childhood Education, 1988. (ERIC Digest).

Katz, Lillian. "What Should Young Children Be Doing?" ***American Educator***, Summer, 1988.

Kavner, Richard. ***Your Child's Vision***. New York: Simon and Schuster, 1985.

Kellogg, Rhoda. ***Analyzing Children's Art***. Mountain View, CA: Mayfield Publishing Co., 1970.

Knight, Michael, et al. ***Teaching Children to Love Themselves: A Handbook for Parents and Teachers of Young Children***. Hillside, NJ: Vision Press, 1989.

Lally, Ronald, et al. "Developmentally Appropriate Care for Children From Birth to Age 3." In Sue Bredekamp (Ed.), ***Developmentally Appropriate Practice in Early Childhood Programs Serving Children From Birth Through Age 8***. Washington, DC: NAEYC, 1987.

Long, Lynette, and Long, Thomas. ***The Handbook for Latchkey Children and Their Parents***. New York: Arbor House, 1983.

Marshall, Hermine. "The Development of Self-Concept." ***Young Children***, Vol. 44, No. 5, July, 1989.

Parker, Jeffrey, and Asher, Steven. "Peer Relations and Later Personal Adjustment: Are Low-Accepted Children At Risk?" ***Psychological Bulletin***, Vol. 102, No. 3, November, 1987.

Peters, Donald, and Willis, Sherry. ***Early Childhood.*** Monterey, CA: Brooks/Cole Publishing Co., Life-Span Human Development Series, 1978.

Piaget, Jean. ***The Psychology of Intelligence***. London: Routledge & Kegan Paul, 1950.

Ross, Dorene, and Bondy, Elizabeth. "Communicating with Parents About Beginning Reading Instruction." ***Childhood Education***, April, 1987.

Segal, Julius. "Compassionate Kids." ***Parents***, September, 1988.

Simmons, Carolyn. "Children Helping Peers: Altruism and Preschool Development." ***Journal of Psychology***, Vol. 115, No. 2, 1983.

Smith, Robert. "Early Childhood Science Education: A Piagetian Perspective." In Janet F. Brown (Ed.), ***Curriculum Planning for Young Children.*** Washington, DC: NAEYC, 1982.

Stipek, D. and Daniels, D. "Declining Perceptions of Competence: A Consequence of Changes in the Child or in the Educational Environment." ***Journal of Educational Psychology***, Vol. 80, 1988.

Temple, Charles, and Gillet, Jean Wallace. ***Language Arts: Learning Processes and Teaching Practices***. Boston: Little, Brown and Co., 1984.

Vail, Priscilla. ***Smart Kids with School Problems: Things to Know and Ways to Help***. New York: E.P. Dutton, 1987.

Wiener, Harold. ***Eyes OK, I'm Okay***. San Rafael, CA: Academic Therapy Publications, 1977.

Wolfgang, Charles, et al. ***Growing and Learning Through Play***. Hightstown, NJ: Instructo/McGraw-Hill, 1981.

Zigler, Edward, and Finn-Stevenson, Matia. ***Children: Development and Social Issues***. Lexington, MA: D.C. Heath, 1987.

Zimbardo, Phillip, and Radl, S. ***The Shy Child: A Parent's Guide to Preventing and Overcoming Shyness From Infancy to Adulthood.*** New York: McGraw-Hill, 1981.

# Related Books and Journal Articles

## Social Development

Adcock, D. and Segal, M. ***Making Friends: Ways of Encouraging Social Development in Young Children.*** Englewood Cliffs, NJ: Prentice-Hall, 1983.

Roopnarine, J. and Honig, A. "The Unpopular Child." ***Young Children***, Vol. 46, No. 6, 1985.

Honig, Alice. "Research in Review: Prosocial Development in Children." ***Young Children***, Vol. 37, No. 5, 1982.

Zimbardo, Phillip. "The Social Disease Called Shyness." ***Psychology Today***, Vol. 8, No. 3, 1975.

## Emotional Development

Berends, Polly Berrien. ***Whole Child/Whole Parent.*** New York: Harper & Row, 1983.

Bernstein, Anne. "Feeling Great (About Myself)." ***Parents***, September, 1982.

Borba, Michele. ***Esteem Builders: A K-8 Self-Esteem Curriculum for Improving Student Achievement, Behavior and School Climate.*** Rolling Hills Estates, CA: Jalmar Press, 1989.

Canfield, Jack. ***Self-Esteem in the Classroom: A Curriculum Guide.*** Pacific Palisades, CA: Self-Esteem Seminars, 1986.

Clemes, Harris and Bean, R. ***How To Raise Children's Self-Esteem.*** Los Angeles: Price, Stern and Sloan, 1986.

Hendrick, Joanne. ***The Whole Child.*** Columbus, OH: Merrill Publishing Co., 1988.

McDaniel, Sandy, and Bielen, Peggy. ***Project Self-Esteem: A Parent Involvement Program for Elementary-Age Children.*** Rolling Hills Estates, CA: B.L. Winch & Associates, 1986.

Purkey, William. ***Self-Concept and School Achievement.*** Englewood Cliffs, NJ: Prentice-Hall, Inc., 1970.

Samuels, Shirley. ***Enhancing Self-Concept in Early Childhood.*** New York: Human Science Press, 1977.

## Physical Development

Gilbert, Anne. ***Teaching the 3 R's through Movement Experiences.*** New York: Macmillian, 1977.

Peck, Judith. ***Leap to the Sun: Learning Through Dynamic Play.*** Englewood Cliffs, NJ: Prentice-Hall, 1979.

Schneider, Tom. ***Everybody's a Winner: A Kid's Guide to New Sports and Fitness.*** Boston: Little, Brown and Co., 1976.

Sullivan, Molly. ***Feeling Strong, Feeling Free: Movement Exploration for Young Children.*** Washington, DC: NAEYC, 1982.

## Intellectual Development

Baratta-Lorton, Mary. ***Workjobs: Activity-Centered Learning for Early Childhood Education.*** Menlo-Park, CA: Addison-Wesley, 1972.

Burns, Marilyn. ***The Book of Think: Or How to Solve a Problem Twice Your Size.*** Boston: Little, Brown & Co., 1976.

Holt, Bess-Gene. ***Science With Young Children.*** Washington, DC: NAEYC, 1977.

Kamii, Constance. ***Numbers in Preschool and Kindergarten.*** Washington DC: NAEYC, 1982.

Kaye, Peggy. ***Games for Math: Playful Ways To Help Your Child Learn Math From Kindergarten to Third Grade.*** New York: Pantheon, 1987.

Schickedanz, Judith. ***More Than ABC's: The Early Stages of Reading and Writing.*** Washington, DC: NAEYC, 1986.

Stenmark, Jean Kerr, et al. ***Family Math.*** Berkley, CA: Lawrence Hall of Science, 1986.

## Audiovisual Materials

### Videotapes

"Raising America's Children"
A series of ten videotapes on children's social skills,
language, special needs, health and play. Available from Frank Porter Graham Child Development Center, DC/TATS MEDIA, University of North Carolina, CB #8040, 300 NCNB Plaza, Chapel Hill, NC 27599-8040.

"Children and Television"
One of 15 videotapes for parents and teachers of children from birth through 5. Available from: South Carolina ETV Network, P.O. Drawer L, Columbia, SC 29250-2712.

"Reading and Young Children"
A discussion with Jan McCarthy about what teachers can say to parents who want their children to learn to read in preschool. Available from NAEYC, 1-800-424-2460.

"Culture and Education of Young Children"
A discussion with Carol Phillips about ways teachers can show respect for cultural diversity. Available from NAEYC.

## *Audiotapes*

"Self-Esteem for the Child"
Six cassette tapes by James Dodson on the ways parents and teachers can maximize self-confidence in children. Write to Vision House Publishers, 2300 Knoll Dr., Ventura, CA 93006.

"Raising Smart Kids: Common Sense, Uncommon Needs"
A talk by Priscilla Vail about the school problems of bright children. Available from Programs For Education/Modern Learning Press, Box 167, Rosemont, NJ 08556, 1-800-627-5867.

"The Basics: Time Play and You"
A discussion by William Page about the role of time, play, and adult participation in child development and learning. Available from Programs for Education/ Modern Learning Press.

## *Newsletters*

"School Success Network Developmental Newsletters"
A series of six newsletters communicating developmental ideas to parents, teachers and community members. Available from The Center for School Success, refer to address above for Programs for Education.

"Raising Kids"
A monthly newsletter which discusses a variety of developmental issues by a range of experts. Available from Raising Kids subscription service, 56 Dudley St., Cambridge, MA 02140, 617-876-1749.

## *Organizations*

American Alliance for Health, Physical Education, Recreation and Dance
1900 Association Drive
Reston, VA 22091
American Optometric Association
700 Chippewa Street
St. Louis, MO 63119

Council on Interracial Books for Children
1841 Broadway
New York, NY 10023
(Interracial Books for Children Bulletin)

National Council for Self-Esteem
P.O. Box 5700
Lincoln, NE 68505

# Chapter 2

## *References*

Armstrong, Thomas. ***In Their Own Way***. New York: St. Martin's Press, 1987.

Benson, Herbert. ***The Relaxation Response***. New York: Morrow, 1975.

Dreyer, Sharon. ***The Bookfinder: A Guide to Children's Literature About the Needs and Problems of Youth Aged 2-15***. Circle Pines, MN: American Guidance Service, 1981.

Elkind, David. ***The Hurried Child***. Reading, MA: Addison-Wesley, 1988.

Fassler, Joan. ***Helping Children Cope: Mastering Stress through Books and Stories***. New York: Free Press, 1978.

Gardner, D.P. and Larsen, Y.W. "A Nation At Risk." National Commission on Excellence in Education. Washington, DC: U.S. Department of Education, 1983.

General Mills American Family Report. ***Families at Work — Strengths and Strains***. Minneapolis: General Mills, 1981.

Halpern, Steven. ***Lullabies and Sweet Dreams, The Anti-Frantic Alternative***. Corte Madera, CA: Halpern Sounds, 1982.

Hoffman, Carol. ***Curriculum Gone Astray: When Push Came to Shove***. Lancaster, PA: Technomic Publishing Co., 1987.

Hyson, Marion C. "'Playing with Kids All Day': Job Stress in Early Childhood Education." ***Young Children***, Vol. 37, No. 2, January, 1982.

Jackson, Charles and Shaughnessy, Michael. "Competitive Sports in the Elementary School: Psychological and Physical Implications." ERIC Document 281 613, 1984.

Kavner, Richard. ***Your Child's Vision***. New York: Simon and Schuster, 1985.

Kuczen, Barbara. ***Childhood Stress: How to Raise a Healthier, Happier Child***. New York: Dell Publishing Co., 1987.

Mann, Sandra Rodman. Quoted in Elin McCoy, "Where Have All the Children Gone?" ***Parents***, Vol. 61, No. 5, May, 1986.

McGuire, Jack. ***Creative Storytelling: Choosing, Inventing and Sharing Tales for Children***. New York: McGraw-Hill, 1985.

Micheli, Lyle. "Overuse Injuries in Children's Sports: The Growth Factor." ***Orthopedic Clinics of North America***, Vol. 14, No. 2, April, 1983.

Murdock, Maureen. ***Spinning Inward: Using Guided Imagery With Children***. Culver City, CA: Peace Press, 1982.

Orlick, Terry and Botterill. ***Every Kid Can Win***. Chicago: Nelson-Hall, 1977.

Orlick, Terry. ***The Second Cooperative Sports & Games Handbook***. New York: Pantheon, 1982.

Packard, Vance. ***Our Endangered Children: Growing Up in a Changing World***. New York: Little, Brown and Co., 1983.

Piper, Francesca. "Stress Management Techniques for Young Children." ERIC document: ED 299 052, 1988.

Plum, Lorraine. ***Flights of Fancy: Ideas and Activities to Foster the Development of Imagination, Relaxation, and Self-Concept***. (tape and book). Carthage, IL: Good Apple Publishing Co., 1980.

***National PTA 88: The PTA Back to School Guide for Parents***. "Getting Physical: A Healthy Attitude Toward Exercise." The National PTA, 1988.

Rapoport, Robert, and Rapoport, Rhona. ***Dual Career Families Re-examined: New Generations of Work and Family***. New York: Harper Colophon, 1976.

Rutter, Michael. "Protective Factors in Children's Responses to Stress and Disadvantage." In M.W. Kent & J.E. Rolf, (Eds.), ***Primary Prevention of Psychopathology, Vol. 3, Promoting Social Competence and Coping in Children***. Hanover, NH: University Press of New England, 1979.

Selye, Hans. ***The Stress of Life***. New York: McGraw-Hill, 1978.

Scott, Louise Binder. ***Quiet Times: Relaxation Techniques for Early Childhood***. Minneapolis: T.S. Denison & Co., 1986.

Singer, Jerome and Singer, Dorothy. "Television Viewing and Aggressive Behavior in Preschool Children: A Field Study." ***Forensic Pathology and Psychiatry***, Vol. 347, 1980.

Tower, Roni Beth, et al. "Differential Effects of Television Programming on Preschoolers' Cognition, Imagination, and Social Play." ***American Journal of Orthopsychiatry***, Vol. 49, No. 2, 1979.

White, L. "Sports Training Injuring Children." ***Boston Globe***, February 11, 1985.

## *Related Books and Journal Articles*

### *Emotional Stress*

Curran, Dolores. ***Stress and the Healthy Family***. New York: Winston Press, 1985.

Doyle, Patricia and Behrens, David. ***The Child in Crisis***. New York: McGraw-Hill, 1986.

Honig, Alice. "Research in Review. Stress and Coping in Children." ***Young Children***, Part 1, Vol. 41, No. 4, May, 1986; Part 2, Vol. 41, No. 5, July, 1986.

Humphrey, J.H. ***Controlling Stress in Children***. Springfield, IL: C.E. Thomas Publishing Co., 1985.

Kersey, Katherine. ***Helping Your Child Handle Stress***. Washington, DC: Acropolis, 1985.

Mancus, Diane and Mancus, Phillip. "How is a Moving Van Like a Camel? Creative Strategies for Helping a Child Deal With Anxiety." ERIC Document: ED 280 599, 1987.

Medeiros, Donald, et al. ***Children Under Stress: How to Help With the Every Day Stresses of Childhood***. Englewood Cliffs: Prentice-Hall, 1983.

Monroe, Marian. "Families, Day Care, and Stress." ERIC Document: ED 206 383, January, 1982.

Procaccini, Joseph and Kiefaber, Mark. ***Parent Burnout***. New York: Doubleday, 1987.

Ruta, Suzanne. "Why Do You Love Us? Are We Your Status Symbol?" ***Working Mother***, September, 1986.

Saunders, Antoinette and Remsberg, Bonnie. ***The Stress-Proof Child***. New York: Signet, 1986.

Segal, Julius. "Why Children Need Their Childhood." ***PTA Today***, Vol. 10, No. 4, February, 1985.

Swick, Kevin. ***Stress and Teaching***. West Haven, CT: NEA Professional Library, 1989.

Youngs, B. ***Stress in Children***. New York: Avon, 1985.

## *Bibliotherapy*

Jalongo, Mary Renck. "Bibliotherapy: Literature to Promote Socio-emotional Growth." ***Reading Teacher***, April, 1983.

Jalongo, Mary Renck. "Using Crisis-Oriented Books with Young Children." In Janet Brown McCracken (Ed.), ***Reducing Stress in Young Children's Lives***. Washington, DC: NAEYC, 1986.

## Physical Stress

McKeag, Douglas. "Sports and the Young Athlete: A Family Practice Perspective." ERIC document: ED 194 463, March, 1981.

Micheli, Lyle. "Preventing Youth Sports Injuries." ***JOPERD***, August, 1985.

Moore, Dorothy. "The Winning Alternative: Solving the Dilemma of the Win/Lose Syndrome." ***Childhood Education***, Vol. 62, No. 3, Jan./Feb., 1986.

O'Neill, Daniel and Micheli, Lyle. "Overuse Injuries in the Young Athlete." ***Clinics in Sports Medicine***, Vol. 7, No. 3, July, 1988.

Seefeldt, Vern. "Handbook for Youth Sports Coaches." ERIC Document: ED 289 870, May, 1988.

## Television

Eron. L. and Huesmann, L. "Television as a Source of Maltreatment of Children." ***School Psychology Review***, Vol. 16, No. 2, 1987.

Lappe, Frances. ***What to Do after You Turn Off the TV***. New York: Ballantine, 1985.

Mander, Jerry. ***Four Arguments for the Elimination of Television***. New York: Morrow, 1978.

Winn, Marie. ***The Plug-In Drug***. New York: Viking, 1985.

# Audiovisual Materials

## Audiotapes

"Kiddie QR: A Choice for Children"
Stress reduction program for children age 4-9; four audio cassettes and four booklets. Write to: QR Publications, 119 Forest Dr., Wethersfield, CT 06109.

"Flights of Fancy: Ideas and Activities to Foster the Development of Relaxation and Self-Concept"
Cassette tape and book. Write to Good Apple Activity Books for Elementary Grades, Good Apple, Inc., Box 299, Carthage, IL 62321.

"Self-Management Tapes"
Cassette tapes using imagery. Write to 1534 Oakstream, Houston, TX 77043.

"Developmental Parenting"
Three cassette tapes by Dr. Anthony J. Coletta on the topics of "Reducing Childhood Stress," "Reducing Parent Stress," and "Reducing School Stress." Write to Programs for Education/ Modern Learning Press, PO Box 167, Rosemont, NJ 08556.

### *Videotapes*

"Coping With Stress"
A videotape suggesting ways to handle family stress. Write to Frank Porter Graham Child Development Center, University of North Carolina, CB #8040, 300 NCNB Plaza, Chapel Hill, NC 27599-8040.

### *Organizations*

Action for Children's Television
20 University Rd.
Cambridge, MA 02138

The American Institute of Stress
124 Park Ave.
Yonkers, NY 10703

Children's Defense Fund
122 C Street, NW
Washington, DC 20001

Parental Stress Inc.
654 Beacon St.
Boston, MA 12215

Preschool Stress Relief Project
P.O. Box 42481, SW
Atlanta GA 30311

## Chapter 3

### *References*

Briggs, Dorothy Corkille. ***Your Child's Self-Esteem***. Garden City, NY: Doubleday, 1975.
Dobson, James. ***The Strong-Willed Child: Birth Through Adolescence***. Wheaton, IL: Tyndale House, 1988.

Dobson, James. ***Parenting Isn't for Cowards: Dealing Confidently with the Frustrations of Child-Rearing***. Dallas: Word Publishing, 1987.

Canter, Lee. "Viewpoint 1. Assertive Discipline and the Search for the Perfect Classroom." ***Young Children***, Vol. 43, No. 2, 1988.

Chess, Stella and Thomas, Alexander. ***Know Your Child: An Authoritative Guide for Today's Parents***. New York: Basic Books, 1987.

Fraiberg, Selma. ***The Magic Years: Understanding and Handling the Problems of Early Childhood***. New York: C.E. Scribner's Sons, 1959.

Hitz, R. "Viewpoint 2. Assertive Discipline: A Response to Canter." ***Young Children***, Vol. 43, No. 2, 1988.

Kiley, Dan. ***The Peter Pan Syndrome: Men Who Have Never Grown Up***. New York: Dodd, Mead, & Co., 1983.

Lewis, Jerry. ***No Single Thread: Psychological Health In Family Systems***. New York: Brunner/Mazel, 1976.

Spock, Benjamin. "How Not to Bring up a Bratty Child." ***Redbook***, February, 1974.
Turecki, Stanley. ***The Difficult Child***. New York: Bantam Books, 1985.

## *Related Books and Journal Articles*

Bates, J.E. "The Concept of Difficult Temperament." ***Merrill-Palmer Quarterly***, Vol. 26, No. 4, October, 1980.

Buss, A.H. and Plomin, R.A. ***A Temperamental Theory of Personality***. New York: Wiley, 1975.

Coles, Robert. ***Privileged Ones***. (Vol. 5 of ***Children Of Crisis***). Boston: Little, Brown, 1977.

Coles, Robert. "What Makes Children Grow up Good?" ***U.S. Catholic***, August, 1979.

Curran, D. ***Traits of a Healthy Family***. New York: Ballantine, 1983.

Gardner, H. G. ***Developmental Psychology***. Boston: Little, Brown, 1981.

Gesell, Arnold. "The Development of Personality: Molding Your Child's Character." ***The Delineator***, April, 1924.

McDevitt, S.C. and Carey, W.B. "The Measurements of Temperaments in 3-7 Year Old Children." ***Journal of Child Psychology and Psychiatry***, Vol. 19, No. 3, July, 1978.

Powell, M. ***Assessment and Management of Developmental Changes and Problems in Children***. St. Louis: Mosby, 1981.

Soderman, Anne K. "Dealing with Difficult Young Children: Strategies for Teachers and Parents." ***Young Children***, Vol. 40, No. 5, July, 1985.

Stinnett, N. ***Building Family Strength***. Lincoln, NE: University of Nebraska Press, 1979.

Thomas, Alexander and Chess, Stella. ***Temperament and Development***. New York: Brunner/Mazel, 1977.

Thomas, Alexander, et al. ***Temperament and Behavior Disorders in Children***. New York: New York University Press, 1968.

Thomas, Alexander, et al. "The Reality of Difficult Temperament." ***Merrill-Palmer Quarterly***, Vol. 28, No. 1, January, 1982.

York, Phyllis, et al. ***Tough Love***. Garden City, NY: Doubleday, 1982.

## *Audiovisual Materials*

### *Videotapes*

"Early Childhood STEP Video."
The STEP (Systematic Training for Effective Parenting) program includes a video which allows parents to observe the methods described in the handbook, ***Parenting Young Children***. Write to American Guidance Service, P.O. Box 99, Publishers' Building, Circle Pines, MN 55014-1796.

"Active Parenting Video Tape."
"Drug-Free Kids"

"Self-esteem, Discipline and Parenting in the 80's"
The above three videos are available as part of the Active Parenting Program. Along with these tapes, also available are a leader's guide, handbook, action guide, and book, ***Active Parenting: Teaching Courage, Cooperation and Responsibility*** by Michael Popkin. Write to Active Parenting, 4669 Roswell Road, NE, Atlanta, GA 30342.

"Discipline: Appropriate Guidance of Young Children"
For teachers and parents, this videotape illustrates the ways positive guidance of young children leads to healthy social and emotional development. Available from NAEYC.

## *Audiotapes*

"How To Talk So Kids Will Listen & Listen So Kids Will Talk"
Adele Faber and Elaine Mazlish have developed a parenting program designed to improve communication skills. The program is comprised of audio tapes, chairperson's guide, participant's workbook, and books such as ***Siblings Without Rivalry***. Write to Negotiation Institute, 230 Park Ave., New York, NY 10169.

"The Strong-Willed Child"
"Parenting Isn't for Cowards"
"Shaping the Will Without Breaking the Spirit"
These audiotapes by psychologist James Dobson describe practical ways to manage the behavior of temperamentally difficult children. Contact Focus on the Family, Pomona CA 91799.

## *Newsletters*

"Parent and Preschooler Newsletter"
Each monthly issue discusses pertinent topics such as "Understanding Your Child's Temperament," "Dealing with Discipline," "Setting Limits," and "Harmony Among Siblings." Write to Betty Farber, Preschool Publications, P.O. Box 1851, Garden City, NY 11530-0816.

"Developments"
An informative newsletter covering a wide array of child development topics. Write to Terry Turner, Frank Porter Graham Center, Highway 54 Bypass-West, Chapel Hill, NC 27514.

## *Organizations*

The Difficult Child Program
Beth Israel Medical Center
10 Nathan D. Perlman Place
New York, NY 10003

Family Resource Coalition
230 No. Michigan Ave.
Suite 1625
Chicago, IL 60601

Parents Anonymous
6733 South Sepulveda Blvd.
Suite 270
Los Angeles, CA 90045

# Chapter 4

## *References*

***AGS Early Screening Profiles***. Circle Pines, MN: American Guidance Service, 1990.

Bracken, Bruce A. "Observing the Assessment Behavior of Preschool Children." In Kathleen Paget and Bruce Bracken (Eds.), ***The Psychoeducational Assessment of Preschool Children***. New York: Grune & Stratton, 1983.

Bredekamp, Sue and Shepard, Lorrie. "How Best To Protect Children From Inappropriate School Expectations, Practices, and Policies." ***Young Children***, Vol. 44, No. 3, March, 1989.

Brevard County Public Schools. ***Developmental Placement Program Evaluation***. Rockledge, FL: School Board of Brevard County, 1987.

Broward County School Board, Department of Research. "Prefirst Grade: A Longitudinal Study (1982-1986)." Department of Early Childhood Education, Fort Lauderdale, FL, 1987.

Bjorkland, David and Bjorkland, Barbara. "Is Your Child Ready for School?" ***Parents***, Vol. 63, No. 6, June, 1988.

Bruner, Jerome. ***Towards a Theory of Instruction***. Cambridge: Harvard University Press, 1966.

Chase, Joan. "Impact of Grade Retention on Primary School Children." ***Journal of Psychology***. Vol. 70, 1968.

Conval Valley Regional Schools "Longitudinal Study of 353 Students, Grades Four, Five and Six." , Temple, NH: Temple Elementary School, 1976.

de Hirsch, Katrina. "Potential Educational Risks." ***Childhood Education***. December, 1964.

Educational Research Service. "Kindergarten Programs and Practices in Public Schools." ***Principal***, Vol. 65, 1986.

Elkind, David. ***All Grown Up & No Place to Go***. Reading, MA: Addison-Wesley, 1984.

Epstein, Herman. "Growth Spurts During Brain Development: Implications for Educational Policy." In J.S. Chall and A.F. Mirsky (Eds.), ***1978 Yearbook of the National Society for the Study of Education***. Chicago: University of Chicago Press, 1978.

Finlayson, Harry. "The Effect of Nonpromotion Upon the Self-concept of Pupils in the Primary Grades." ERIC Document: 155 556, 1975.

Fischer, Kurt. ***Human Development***. New York: W.H. Freeman and Co., 1984.

Frankenburg, W.F. et al. ***Denver Developmental Screening Test***. Denver, CO: LADOCA Publishing Foundation, 1970.

Gesell Institute of Human Development. ***Gesell Developmental Observation Kindergarten Assessment (Ages 4-6 Years)***. Rosemont, NJ: Programs for Education, 1978.

Grant, Jim. ***I Hate School!*** Rosemont, NJ: Programs for Education/Modern Learning Press, 1986.

Hutt, Corinne. ***Males and Females***. New York: Penguin Books, 1972.

Ilg, Frances L. et al. ***School Readiness: Behavior Tests Used at the Gesell Institute***. New York: Harper & Row, 1978.

Ireton, Harry. ***Preschool Development Inventory***. Order from Behavior Science Systems, Box 1108, Minneapolis, MN; or from American Guidance Service, Circle Pines, MN.

Kagan, Jerome. ***Psychological Research on the Human Infant.*** New York: WT Grant Foundation, 1982.

Landry, Coy L. and Frank, Merlene. "A History of Developmental Placement in St. Charles Parish Public Schools, Luling, Louisiana." In James Uphoff (Ed.), ***Changing to a Developmentally Appropriate Curriculum—Successfully.*** Rosemont, NJ: Programs for Education/Modern Learning Press, 1989.

Lichtenstein, Robert. ***Minneapolis Preschool Screening Instrument.*** Minneapolis, MN: Prescriptive Instruction Center, Minneapolis Public Schools, 1980.

Lichtenstein, Robert and Ireton, Harry. ***Preschool Screening: Identifying Young Children with Developmental and Educational Problems.*** New York: Grune & Stratton, 1984.

Lichtenstein, Robert. "Reanalysis of Research on Early Retention and Extra Year Programs." A paper presented at the 21st Annual Convention of the National Association of School Psychologists. Boston, March, 1988.

Lichtenstein, Robert. "Psychometric Characteristics and Appropriate Use of the Gesell School Readiness Screening Test." ***Early Childhood Research Quarterly***, 1990.

Lichtenstein, Robert. "Kindergarten Screening and Developmental Placement: Rationale, Practice, and Research." Submitted for publication, 1990.

Liddle, Gordon and Long, Dale. "Experimental Room for Slow-Learners. ***Elementary School Journal***, Vol. 59, December, 1958.

McGuinness, Diane. ***When Children Don't Learn: Understanding the Biology and Psychology of Learning Disabilities.*** New York: Basic Books, 1985.

Meisels, Samuel J. and Wiske, Martha S. ***Early Screening Inventory.*** New York: Teachers College Press, Teachers College, Columbia University, 1983.

Meisels, Samuel. ***Developmental Screening in Early Childhood: A Guide.*** Washington, DC: NAEYC, 1985.

Mussen, Paul and Jones, M.C. "Self-Conceptions, Motivations and Interpersonal Attitudes of Late- and Early-Maturing Boys." ***Child Development***, Vol. 28, 1957.

National Association for the Education of Young Children. "Position Statement on Standardized Testing of Young Children 3 Through 8 Years of Age." ***Young Children***, Vol. 43, No. 3, March, 1988.

Nelson, Ben. "Oxford Public Schools, Oxford, N.Y." In James Uphoff (Ed.), ***Changing to a Developmentally Appropriate Curriculum—Successfully***. Rosemont, NJ: Programs for Education/Modern Learning Press, 1989.

Peck, Johanne, et al. ***Kindergarten Policies: What Is Best For Children?*** Washington, DC: NAEYC, 1988.

Piaget, Jean. ***The Psychology of Intelligence***. London: Routledge & Kegan Paul, 1950.

Rose, J.S. et al. "A Fresh Look At the Retention-Promotional Controversy." ***Journal of School Psychology***, Vol. 21, 1983.

Sandoval, Jonathan and Fitzgerald, Phyllis. "A High School Follow-Up of Children Who Were Nonpromoted or Attended a Junior First Grade." ***Psychology in the Schools***, Vol. 22, April, 1985.

Sava, Sam. "Development, Not Academics." ***Young Children***, Vol. 42, No. 3, March, 1987.

Shepard, Lorrie A. and Smith, Mary Lee. "Synthesis of Research on School Readiness and Kindergarten Retention." ***Educational Leadership***, Vol. 44, November, 1986.

Shepard, Lorrie A. and Smith, Mary Lee. ***Boulder Valley Kindergarten Study: Retention Practices and Retention Effects***. Boulder, CO: Boulder Valley Public Schools, 1985.

Soderman, Anne K. "Formal Education for Four-Year Olds? That Depends..." ***Young Children***, Vol. 39, July, 1984.

Sprinthall, Norman A. and Theis-Sprinthall, Lois. "The Need for Theoretical Frameworks in Educating Teachers." In ***The Education of Teachers: A Look Ahead***. White Plains, NY: Longman, 1983.

Sweitzer, Susan L. Quoted in "Gesell Institute Is Facing Uncertain Future In Wake of Budget Woes, Testing Questions." ***Education Week***, Vol. 9, No. 8, October 25, 1989.

Tanner, James. "Growth and Development of the Brain." In J. Tanner, ***Foetus Into Man***. Cambridge: Harvard University Press, 1978.

Uphoff, James, et al. ***Summer Children: Ready or Not For School***. Middletown, OH: J & J Publishing Co., 1986.

Uphoff, James. "Proving Your Program Works." ***School Success Network Newsletter***, Issue 8, Fall, 1989. Rosemont, NJ: Programs for Education/Modern Learning Press.

Uphoff, James. ***School Readiness and Transition Programs: Real Facts From Real Schools***. Rosemont, NJ: Programs For Education, 1990.

Walker, Richard. "The Gesell Screening Examination: Psychometric Properties." Gesell Institute of Human Development, New Haven, CT. Submitted for publication, 1990.

***Wechsler Preschool and Primary Scale of Intelligence***. San Antonio, TX: Psychological Corporation.

Wiener, Gerald. "Scholastic Achievement at Age 12-13 of Prematurely Born Infants." ***Journal of Special Education***, Vol. 2, No. 3, 1968.

Wood, Robert, et al. ***A Notebook for Teachers: Making Changes in the Elementary Curriculum***. Greenfield, MA: Northeast Foundation for Children, 1986.

Wood, Robert. "The Developmental Effect." ***Journal of Learning Disabilities***, Vol. 17, No. 4, January, 1984.

Zigler, Edward and Finn-Stevenson, Matia. ***Children: Development and Social Issues***. Lexington, MA: D.C. Heath, 1987.

## *Related Books and Journal Articles*

Ames, L.B. "Ready Or Not: How Birthdays Leave Some Children Behind." ***American Educator***, Summer, 1986.

Anastasiow, N.J., et al. ***Identifying the Developmentally Delayed Child***. Baltimore: University Park Press, 1982.

Barnes, K.E. ***Preschool Screening: The Measurement and Prediction of Children At-Risk***. Springfield, IL: Charles Thomas, 1982.

Bracken, B. ***Psychoeducational Assessment of Preschool Children***. Boston: Allyn and Bacon, 1990.

Buros, O.K. (Ed.) ***The Tenth Mental Measurements Yearbook***. Lincoln, NE: University of Nebraska Press, 1989.

Charlesworth, R. "'Behind' Before They Start? Deciding How to Deal With the Risk of Kindergarten 'Failure'." ***Young Children***, Vol. 44, No. 3, March, 1989.

Elkind, David. "Readiness for Kindergarten." ***Young Children***, Vol. 42, No. 3, March, 1987.

Grant, J. (Ed.) ***Book of Parent Pages***. Rosemont, NJ: Programs for Education/ Modern Learning Press, 1988.

Gredler, G. "Transition Classes: A Viable Alternative for the At-Risk Child?" ***Psychology in the Schools***, Vol. 21, October, 1984.

Hills, T.W. "Screening for School Entry." ERIC Digest: ERIC Clearinghouse on Elementary and Early Childhood Education, 1987.

Kaufman, N. "Review of Gesell School Readiness Test." In J.V. Michael (Ed.) ***Ninth Mental Measurements Yearbook***. Lincoln, NE: Buros Institute of Mental Measurements, 1985.

Meisels, S. "High Stakes Testing." ***Educational Leadership***, April, 1989.

Nurss, J.R. "Readiness for Kindergarten." ERIC Digest: ERIC Clearinghouse on Elementary and Early Childhood Education, 1987.

Roberts, F. "Is Your Child Ready for Kindergarten?" ***Parents***, August, 1984.

Robinson, Sandra. "School Entrance Age and the Three R's: Research, Reality and Recommendations." ***Kappa Delta Phi Record***, Fall, 1986.

Solem, M. R. "Junior First Grade: A Year to Get Ready." ***Phi Delta Kappan***, Vol. 63, No. 4, December, 1981.

Turley, C.C. "A Study of Elementary School Children for Whom a Second Year of Kindergarten Was Recommended." ***California Reader***, March/April, 1982.

Wood, R. "Extending Appropriate Practices in the Elementary School." ***Education Week***, Vol. 12, No. 29, April 13, 1988.

## *Audiovisual Materials*

### *Audiotapes*

"Implementing a Developmental Program" by Robert Johnson

Discusses the development of a school philosophy, needs assessment committee, plan of action and inservice training. Write to Programs for Education/Modern Learning Press, Rosemont, NJ 08556.

"Jim Grant Live" by Jim Grant
Discusses school readiness and why some children do not succeed in school. Write to Programs for Education.

## Videotapes

"Questions Parents Ask" by Gwen Webb
The 16 questions most frequently asked by parents about school readiness are presented and discussed. Write to Programs for Education.

"Do You Know Where Your Child Is? What Every Parent Should Know About School Success" by Jim Grant
Discusses the concepts of individual rates of growth, overplacement, and "developmental youngness." Write to Programs for Education.

"Ready Or Not Here I Come/An Evaluation of the Whole Child"
An explanation of the use of developmental criteria to place children in school, and a demonstration of a complete screening of a 5 year old. Write to Programs for Education.

"Culture and Education of Young Children"
A discussion with early childhood educator Carol Phillips about the importance of showing respect for cultural diversity and sensitivity to differences in backgrounds. Write to NAEYC in Washington, DC.

## Newsletters and Journals

ERIC/ECE Newsletter
805 W. Pennsylvania Ave.
Urbana, IL 61801

Early Childhood Research Quarterly
NAEYC
Ablex Publishing Co.
355 Chesnut St.
Norwood, NJ 07648

## Organizations

Center for School Success (Information on School Readiness)
Rosemont, NJ 08556

Early Prevention of School Failure Program
114 N. Second Street
Peotone Schools
Peotone, IL 60468

Northeast Foundation for Children
P.O. Box 1024
Greenfield, MA 01302

Gesell Institute of Human Development
310 Prospect St.
New Haven, CT 06511

# Chapter 5

## References

***A Nation at Risk: The Imperative for Educational Reform.*** (Richard Anderson) Washington, DC: National Commission on Excellence in Education, 1983.

Argondizza, Maizie. ***Big Book for Educators: Developmentally Appropriate Practice: A Guide to Change.*** Augusta, ME: Early Elementary Office, State House Station, 1987.

Association for Supervision and Curriculum Development. "How Special Should the Special Ed Curriculum Be?" ***Curriculum Update***, September, 1988.

Bennett, William J. ***First Lessons: A Report on Elementary Education in America.*** Washington, DC: Superintendent of Documents, U.S. Government Printing Office, 1985.

Blake, H. ***Creating a Learning Centered Classroom.*** New York: Hart Publishing, 1977.

Bredekamp, Sue. (Ed.) ***Developmentally Appropriate Practice in Early Childhood Programs Serving Children From Birth Through Age 8.*** Washington, DC: The National Association for the Education of Young Children, 1987.

Burts, Diane, et al. "A Comparison Of Frequencies Of Stress Behaviors Observed In Kindergarten Children In Classrooms With Developmentally Appropriate Versus Developmentally Inappropriate Instructional Practices." ***Early Childhood Research Quarterly*** (in press), 1990.

Carbo, Marie, et al. ***Teaching Students to Read Through Their Individual Learning Styles***. Englewood Cliffs: Prentice-Hall, 1986.

Day, Barbara. ***Early Childhood Education: Creative Learning Activities***. New York: Macmillan, 1988.

Dweck, Carol S. "Motivational Processes Affecting Learning." ***American Psychologist***, Vol. 41, No. 10, October, 1986.

***Education Letter***. "Organizing Classes by Ability." Cambridge: Harvard University Free Press, Vol. 3, No. 4, July, 1987.

Elkind, David. "Superbaby Syndrome Can Lead to Elementary School Burnout." ***Young Children***, Vol. 42, No. 3, 1987.

Elkind, David. "The Resistance to Developmentally Appropriate Educational Practice with Young Children: The Real Issue." In Cynthia Warger (Ed.) ***A Resource Guide to Public School Early Childhood Programs***. Alexandria, VA: Association for Supervision and Curriculum Development, 1988.

Greenman, J. ***Caring Spaces, Learning Places***. Redmond, WA: Exchange Press, 1988.

Haskins, Ron. "Public School Aggression Among Children With Varying Day Care Experience." ***Child Development***, Vol. 56, 1985.

Hoffman, Carol. ***Curriculum Gone Astray: When Push Came To Shove***. Lancaster, PA: Technomic Publishing Co., 1987.

Hyson, Marion, Hirsh-Pasek, Kathryn, and Rescorla, Leslie. "Academic Environments in Preschool: Do They Create Challenge or Pressure?" ***Early Education and Development***. In Press, 1990.

Kantrowitz, Barbara and Wingert, Pat. "How Kids Learn." ***Newsweek***, April 17, 1989.

Katz, Lillian G. "What Should Young Children Be Doing." ***American Educator***, Vol. 12, No. 2, Summer, 1988.

Katz, Lillian G. and Chard, Sylvia C. ***Engaging Children's Minds: The Project Approach***. Norwood, NJ: Ablex.

Melle, Marge and Wilson, Fern. "Balanced Instruction Through an Integrated Curriculum." ***Educational Leadership***, Vol. 41, April, 1984.

McGarry, Thomas. "Integrating Learning for Young Children." ***Educational Leadership***, November, 1986.

National Association of State Boards of Education. ***Right From the Start***. Alexandria, VA: NASBE, 1988.

Papert, Seymour. ***Mindstorms: Children, Computers, and Powerful Ideas***. New York: Basic Books, 1980.

Routman, Regie. ***Transitions: From Literature to Literacy***. Portsmouth, NH: Heinemann, 1988.

Ruthman, Paul. "France." In J. Downing (Ed.) ***Comparative Reading***. New York: Macmillian, 1973.

Sava, Sam. "Development, Not Academics." ***Young Children***. Vol. 42, No. 3, 1987.

Schweinhart, Lawrence and Weikart, David. "Consequences of Three Preschool Curriculum Models Through Age 15." ***Early Childhood Research Quarterly***, Vol. 1, 1986.

Severeide, Rebecca. "A Self-Study Document for Prekindergarten Through Second Grade." Portland, Oregon Public Schools, 1988.

Strickland, Dorothy S. and Morrow, Lesley Mandel. (Eds.) ***Emerging Literacy: Young Children Learn to Read and Write***. Newark, DE: International Reading Association, 1989.

Temple, Charles A. et al. ***The Beginnings of Writing***. Boston: Allyn and Bacon, 1982.

Wisconsin Center for Educational Research. "Ability Grouping Can Hurt Achievement." ***News***, Madison, WI: Wisconsin Center for Educational Research, Summer, 1984.

Wood, Robert. ***A Notebook for Teachers***. Greenfield, MA: Northeast Foundation for Children, 1986.

# Related Books and Journal Articles

Armstrong, Thomas. ***In Their Own Way***. New York: St. Martin's Press, 1987.

Barbe, Walter B. and Swassing, Raymond. ***Teaching Through Modality Strengths: Concepts and Practices***. Columbus, OH: Zaner-Bloser, 1979.

Becher, R. "Parent Involvement: A Review of Research and Principles of Successful Practice." ERIC Document: 247 032, 1987.

Butler, Dorothy and Clay, Marie. ***Reading Begins At Home***. Portsmouth, NH: Heinemann, 1983.

Clay, Marie. ***Writing Begins at Home***. Portsmouth, NH: Heinemann, 1987.

Coletta, Anthony and Coletta, Kathleen. ***Preschool Curriculum Library: Year 'Round Activities for Two, Three, and Four Year-Olds***. West Nyack, NY: Center for Applied Research in Education, 1986.

Dunn, Rita and Dunn, Ken. ***Teaching Students Through Their Individual Learning Styles: A Practical Approach***. Reston, VA: Reston Publishing Co., 1978.

Early Childhood and Literacy Development Committee for the International Reading Association. "Literacy Development and Pre-First Grade: A Joint Statement of Concerns About Present Practices in Pre-First Grade Reading Instruction and Recommendations for Improvement." ***Young Children***, May, 1986.

Gregorc, Anthony. "Learning Style/Brain Research: Harbinger of an Emerging Psychology." In ***Student Learning Styles and Brain Behavior***. Reston, VA: National Association of Secondary School Principals, 1982.

Hatch, J. Amos and Freeman, Evelyn. "Who's Pushing Whom? Stress and Kindergarten." ***Phi Delta Kappan***, October, 1988.

Seefeldt, Carol. ***The Early Childhood Curriculum: A Review of Current Research***. New York: Teachers College Press, 1987.

Wadsworth, Barry. ***Piaget for the Classroom Teacher***. New York: Longman, 1978.

Williams, Connie and Kamii, Constance. "How Do Children Learn by Handling Objects?" ***Young Children***, November, 1986.

# Audiovisual Materials

## Videotapes

"Places To Start: Implementing the Developmental Classroom."
Discusses how to implement developmentally-effective practices in K-3 classrooms. Available from the Northeast Foundation for Children, P.O. Box 1024, Greenfield, MA 01302.

"Appropriate Curriculum for Young Children: The Role of the Teacher"
Illustrates the role of the adult in helping children learn in a play-oriented environment. Available from NAEYC.

"Curriculum for Preschool and Kindergarten"
A discussion with Dr. Lillian Katz about appropriate learning experiences for four and five year-olds. Available from NAEYC.

"NAEYC's Position on Developmentally Appropriate Practice: A Panel Discussion and Critique."
Barbara Bowman, Patty Calvert, Constance Kamii, Lillian Katz, and David Weikart debate DAP. Available from NAEYC.

"Learning — A Matter of Style"
Learning style expert Rita Dunn explains her research on responding to individual learning preferences. Available from the Association for Supervision and Curriculum Development, 1250 N. Pitt Street, Alexandria, VA 22314-1403.

"Curriculum for Four-Year Olds"
Describes a cognitive-based curriculum for young children. Available from South Carolina Educational TV, P.O. Drawer L, Columbia, SC 29250-2712.

"Looking At Young Children: Observing in Early Childhood Settings"
Based on the book, ***The Classroom Observer***, by Ann Boehm, this videotape uses everyday examples to illustrate the basic principles of observing young children. Available from Teachers College Press, P.O. Box 939, Wolfeboro, New Hampshire 03894.

## Audiotapes

"The Responsive Classroom" by Robert Wood
A keynote address to 500 early childhood educators explores the significance of play in children's learning and the importance of the "social" curriculum. Available from the Northeast Foundation for Children, P.O. Box 1024, Greenfield, MA 01302.

## Newsletters

"The Whole Idea" (Four issues per year/no charge)
The Wright Group
10949 Technology Place
San Diego, CA 92127

"Whole Language Newsletter"
Whole Language
123 Newkirk Rd.
Richmond Hill, Ontario, Canada L4C 3G5

## Organizations

Association for Childhood Education International
11141 Georgia Ave.
Suite 200
Wheaton, MD 20902

Association for Supervision and Curriculum Development
1250 N. Pitt Street
Alexandria, VA 22314-1403

High/Scope Educational Research Foundation
600 North River St.
Ypsilanti, MI 48198
(Write for High/Scope Resources)

Learning Styles Network
School of Education and Human Services
St. John's University
Grand Central and Utopia Parkways
Jamacia, NY 11439

National Association for the Education of Young Children (NAEYC)
1834 Connecticut Avenue N.W.
Washington, DC 20009
(Request a catalog of publications, videos, pamphlets and brochures)

National Association of State Boards of Education (NASBE)
Early Childhood Project
701 N. Fairfax St.
Suite 340

Alexandria, VA 22314
(Request a copy of ***Right From the Start***)

National Association of Elementary School Principals
1615 Duke Street
Alexandria, VA 22314
(Request a copy of ***Early Childhood Education and the Elementary School Principal***, written by the Early Childhood Guidelines Committee.)

# Chapter 6

## *References*

Almy, Millie and Genishi, Celia. ***Ways of Studying Children***. New York: Teachers College Press, 1979.

American Federation of Teachers (AFT). "Standardized Testing in Kindergarten. 1988 Convention Policy Resolution." In ***AFT Convention Report***. Washington, DC: July, 1988.

***American Teacher***. "Forget the Tests, the Teacher Knows Best." News and Trends, September, 1989.

Barbe, Walter, et al. ***Basic Skills in Kindergarten: Foundations for Formal Learning***. Columbus, OH: Zaner-Bloser, 1980.

Boehm, Ann and Weinberg, Richard. ***The Classroom Observer: A Guide for Developing Observation Skills***. New York: Teachers College Press, 1977.

Chittenden, Edward and Courtney, Rosalea. "Assessment of Young Children's Reading: Documentation as an Alternative to Testing." In Kenneth Goodman, et al. (Eds.) ***The Whole Language Evaluation Book***. Portsmouth, NH: Heinemann, 1989.

Clay, Marie. ***The Early Detection of Reading Difficulties***. Portsmouth, NH: Heinemann, 1979.

Clay, Marie. ***What Did I Write?*** Portsmouth, NH: Heinemann, 1982.

Coletta, Anthony and Coletta, Kathleen. ***Preschool Curriculum Library: Year 'Round Activities for Two, Three and Four Year-Old Children***. West Nyack, NY: Center for Applied Research in Education (Prentice-Hall), 1986.

Durkin, Dolores. "Testing in the Kindergarten." ***The Reading Teacher***, Vol. 40, No. 8, April, 1987.

Graves, Donald. **Writing: Teachers and Children at Work**. Portsmouth, NH: Heinemann, 1983.

Hood, Wendy. "If the Teacher Comes Over, Pretend It's a Telescope." In Kenneth Goodman, et al.(Eds.) ***The Whole Language Evaluation Book***. Portsmouth, NH: Heinemann, 1989.

Kamii, Constance (Ed.) **Achievement Testing in the Early Grades: The Games Grown-Ups Play**. Washington, DC: NAEYC, 1990.

Katz, Lillian G. "Dispositions in Early Childhood Education." ***ERIC/EECE Bulletin***, Vol. 18, No. 2, 1985.

Lay-Dopyera, Margaret. ***Report: Observational Documentation of Children's Progress in Kindergarten and Primary Grades***. Syracuse, NY: Syracuse University, 1989.

Morrow, Lesley Mandel. **Literacy Development in the Early Years**. Englewood Cliffs, NJ: Prentice Hall, 1989.

National Association for the Education of Young Children. "Position Statement on Standardized Testing of Young Children 3 Through 8 Years of Age." ***Young Children***, Vol. 43, No. 3, March, 1988.

National Association for the Education of Young Children. ***Testing of Young Children: Concerns and Cautions*** (Brochure). Washington, DC: NAEYC, 1988.

Routman, Regie. ***Transitions: From Literature to Literacy***. Portsmouth, NH: Heinemann, 1988.

Schweinhart, Lawrence. ***A School Administrator's Guide To Early Childhood Programs***. Ypsilanti, MI: The High Scope Press, 1988.

Seefeldt, Carol. ***Social Studies for the Preschool-Primary Child***. Columbus, OH: Merrill Publishing Co., 1989.

Stallman, Anne C. and Pearson, David. "Formal Measures of Early Literacy." In Lesley Mandel Morrow and Jeffery Smith (Eds.) ***Assessment for Instruction in Early Literacy***. Englewood Cliffs: Prentice-Hall, 1990.

Sulzby, Elizabeth and Teale, William. "Writing development in Early Childhood." In Kenneth Goodman, et al (Eds.) ***The Whole Language Evaluation Book***. Portsmouth, NH: Heinemann, 1989.

## Related Books and Journal Articles

Cryan, John. "Evaluation: Plague or Promise?" ***Childhood Education***, Vol. 62, No. 5, May/June, 1986.

Fennessy, Dennis. "Primary Teachers' Assessment Practices: Some Implications for Teacher Training." ERIC Document: 229 346, 1982.

Genishi, Celia and Dyson, Anne Haas. ***Language Assessment in the Early Years***. Norwood, NJ: Ablex Publishing Co., 1984.

Price, Gary. "Standardized Achievement Tests for Young Children: An Analysis." ERIC Document: 170 020, 1978.

Roberts, Francis. "Testing 1...2...3." ***Parents***, May, 1984.

Strickland, Dorothy and Morrow, Lesley Mandel. "Assessment and Early Literacy." ***The Reading Teacher***, April, 1989.

Teale, William, et al. "Assessing Young Children's Literacy Development." ***The Reading Teacher***, Vol. 40, No. 8, April, 1987.

Wiggins, Grant. "A True Test: Toward More Authentic and Equitable Assessment." **Phi Delta Kappan**, Vol. 70, No. 9, pp. 703-713, 1989.

## Advocacy

Goffin, Stacie. ***Speaking Out: Early Childhood Advocacy***. Washington, DC: NAEYC, 1989.

NAEYC. ***Guiding Principles for the Development and Analysis of Early Childhood Legislation***. Washington, DC: NAEYC, 1989.

## Newsletters

"FairTest Examiner"
A quarterly newsletter published by FairTest National Center (Address below).

*Appendix* D

# Organizations

FairTest National Center for Fair and Open Testing
324 Broadway
Cambridge, MA 02139-1802

ERIC Clearinghouse on Elementary & Early Childhood Education
University of Illinois at Urbana-Champaign
805 W. Pennsylvania Ave.
Urbana, IL 61801

National Conference of State Legislatures
Child Care/Early Education Project
1050 17th St.
Suite 2100
Denver, CO 80265

# Index